What Do **PAGANS** Believe?

Graham Harvey

Granta Books
London

Granta Publications, 2/3 Hanover Yard, Noel Road, London N1 8BE
First published in Great Britain by Granta Books, 2007

Extracts used with kind permission:
Don McLeod, 'Spells and Magic' in Douglas Ezzy (ed.) 2003, *Practising the
Witch's Craft*, Crows Nest, NSW: Allen & Unwin, p. 150. Used by kind
permission of Don McLeod. Gordon MacLellan, 2005, 'Dancing in the
Daylight: A Role for Shamanism in Social and Environmental Change', in Ly de
Angeles, Emma Restall Orr and Thom van Dooren (eds.) *Pagan Visions for a
Sustainable Future*, Woodbury, MN: Llewellyn, p. 194. *The Saga of Eirik the Red*,
translated by Phil Cardew of London South Bank University. Used by kind
permission of Phil Cardew. *The Druid Source Book* by John Matthews (London:
Blandford, 1997). Used by kind permission of Continuum International
Publishing Group. Kenneth Jackson, 1951, *A Celtic Miscellany: Translations from
the Celtic Literatures* (Harmondsworth, Penguin), pp. 143, 164, 173–4. Mary
Oliver, 'Wild Geese' in *Dream Work*, 1986, Atlantic Monthly Press.
Used by kind permission of Atlantic Monthly Press.

A CIP catalogue record for this book is
available from the British Library.

1 3 5 7 9 10 8 6 4 2

ISBN 978-1-86207-837-6

Typeset by M Rules
Printed and bound in Great Britan by
Bookmarque Ltd, Croydon, Surrey

Graham Harvey is a lecturer in Religious Studies at the Open University, UK. He celebrates Pagan festivals mostly with Druid Orders and animist eco-activists, but he also celebrates Jewish festivals with his wife, Molly. His books include *Listening People, Speaking Earth: Contemporary Paganism*, *The Paganism Reader* (co-edited with Chas Clifton) and *Animism*.

The cover image: Relationships with the earth, the sun and all of life are often celebrated among standing stones, themselves treated as living beings. The stones were erected by our ancient ancestors, who like Pagans today honoured the changing seasons and cycles of the cosmos.

SERIES EDITOR: TONY MORRIS

Available now

What Do Astrologers Believe? by Nicholas Campion
What Do Buddhists Believe? by Tony Morris
What Do Christians Believe? by Malcolm Guite
What Do Druids Believe? by Philip Carr-Gomm
What Do Existentialists Believe? by Richard Appignanesi
What Do Greens Believe? by Joe Smith
What Do Jews Believe? by Edward Kessler
What Do Muslims Believe? by Ziauddin Sardar
What Do Zionists Believe? by Colin Shindler

Forthcoming

What Do Catholics Believe? by Leonie Caldecott
What Do Hindus Believe? by Rachel Dwyer

For Molly

Contents

Introduction

While I was writing this book, I took a break to help a neighbour spread some topsoil over her garden. We were chatting about plants when her nephew joined the conversation. After a while he asked what I do for a living. When I told him I'm a lecturer in Religious Studies at the Open University, he responded, 'Ah, well, you know that there's only one religion, don't you?' I expected he would then proclaim his belief in the 'one true god' or assert that all religions lead to the same god. Instead he surprised me by saying, 'The earth is the only religion. Well, maybe the earth and the sun.' He had put into words the starting point of the Pagan religion: the earth and the sun.

Life and living in the world is the focus of Pagan celebration, and the earth and the sun are the ultimate providers of all that we need to live. Not them alone, of course; but fundamentally them. They provide our light, air, food, water, gravity and material constituents. Pagans agree with the scientific explanation of the origins and nature of the cosmos as the product of the laws of evolution. They celebrate and revere the interaction of all beings and the natural forces that impinge on them. Alongside the Pagan belief in the goodness of nature is the belief that magic can help people improve the world. Most Pagans also believe in the existence of deities and other beings, such as ancestors (relatives who have died, some many centuries ago), the four elemental forces of earth, air, water and fire, and faery people. Pagans' everyday engagement with the deities encourages a reverence for nature and a respect for life. In essence, Paganism is about living respectfully as part of a diverse and vibrant planetary community, sometimes aided by magic and always in the company of other living beings: animals, plants, birds, microbes, and perhaps deities and fairies.

In this book, I examine core Pagan beliefs, practices and experiences, and say something about the varieties of Paganism today. I introduce current Pagan priorities which might become more or less important to Pagans in the future, such as an increasing focus on connections to particular places, and recent demands by some Pagans for wider recognition as clergy. Mainly though, I have tried to capture what makes Pagan beliefs both positive and radical – even when they seem to be about entirely ordinary things like sunrises, dances, songs, special places, moonlit nights and topsoil.

1

What is a Pagan?

Pagans celebrate the natural world and encourage a sense of belonging in it. Different Pagan groups and individuals express that understanding in different ways. Some are attracted to the practice of magic (a term I'll explain in more detail later) as a means of adjusting their lives to the cycles of earth, moon, sun and stars. Some express their respect for the world by participating in environmental action.

The term 'Pagan' has been used in a wide variety of ways over the ages. It began as a Latin word meaning the resident of an area, somewhat like the word 'parishioner' today: someone who lives in an area and knows its places of worship (even if they don't always participate in ceremonies there). As more Romans became Christians the term came to mean someone who had not yet converted to the new religion, or worse, someone who wickedly refused to convert. Its meaning later extended to anyone who is not a Christian, Jew or Muslim; someone who does not belong to one of the large religions; even someone who is anti-religious.

Over time, the word 'Pagan' also came to be associated with the countryside. Victorian scholars translated the Latin word as 'country person' or peasant. And with this shift came a new attitude to Paganism. In the nineteenth century, as people moved into industrial cities and many found life increasingly unpleasant, the rural countryside became ever more attractive. Poets and writers such as Keats, Swinburne and Hardy began to write about 'nature' not as a dangerous place in need of salvation and civilization, but as a realm of authenticity and majesty. Natural desires and instincts were a source of creativity and good rather than a cause for repentance. Hardy, for example, enthuses that in remote Dorset villages 'homage to nature, self-adoration, frantic gaieties, fragments of Teutonic rites to divinities whose names are forgotten, have in some way or other survived medieval doctrine.'[1] A Roman Pagan was now imagined romantically as someone who lived in the countryside, in a traditional village, close to the changing seasons, and who relied on and practised fertility rituals. Historically speaking this is inaccurate, but it inspired new thinking about what might be worthy of celebration. When the ancient, indigenous European ways of celebrating the natural world and the ancestral deities were revived in the 1950s, Pagan was a ready and waiting label for this old-new religion.

More recently, Pagans have learnt about classical paganism from academics such as Ronald Hutton and Ken

Dowden, whose emphasis on the original meaning of 'Pagan' – 'an inhabitant of a particular place' – has encouraged a new focus on locality in modern Paganism. A classical Pagan was someone who belonged, someone who celebrated where they lived, someone who knew their local shrines, springs, hills, trees and neighbours, and could trace their descent from local ancestors. These ancient Pagans lived in both urban and rural places; the important thing was belonging to an area.

The shifts in meaning of the word 'Pagan' match trends within the Pagan religion. Initially, Paganism was a Romantic movement of esotericists who visited the countryside or 'wilderness' to find themselves and perform empowering fertility rituals. Not only have Pagans now recovered the value of cities (because *all* the earth is sacred and everywhere is part of nature), but they also increasingly celebrate particular locations (not only Stonehenge and ancient sacred sites but also places near their homes). Some confront threats to environmentally fragile sites, others aid the ecological recuperation of the areas where they live.

Because of the long history of negative associations Pagans often have to explain that they are neither anti-religious nor irreligious. Paganism is simply a different, distinct religion. Pagans celebrate a series of seasonal festivals, perform magical ceremonies, honour various deities, elementals, ancestors and other significant beings, and seek to live ethical and environmentally responsible lives. Because they place so much stress on the active celebration of the natural world theirs is often categorized as a 'nature religion'. Unlike some other belief systems, Paganism does not teach that the world is a place from which people might need saving or liberating so that they can go to heaven or nirvana. Rather, it encourages people to become more intimate with their world and to celebrate their sensual belonging in it. Pagans are at home in the world as it is.

Every now and again Pagans are accused – normally by evangelical Christians – of worshipping the devil. In fact, Pagans do not believe in evil or in a devil. They acknowledge that life can be tough, dangerous and extremely cruel at times. When Pagans celebrate the natural world they do not ignore the existence of predators. Violent deaths and atrocities do not lead Pagans to believe in evil but, rather, to seek ways to work for just resolutions and the end of conflict.

Every religion has a particular activity that reveals what is at its heart. For Buddhists it might be sitting in meditation, for Christians taking Communion, for Jews lighting candles at the beginning of Shabbat. The celebration of natural cycles in seasonal festivals is the core activity which unites all Pagans. Some might stand in an ancient stone circle watching the sun rise. Some join friends, energetically chanting and dancing in a circle under a full moon. The style in which they celebrate, the kind of magic they perform during these festivals, and the ancestors they honour (Celts, Lithuanians, Saxons and others) define the subdivisions within the Pagan tradition.

MARY OLIVER, 'WILD GEESE'

'You do not have to be good.
You do not have to walk on your knees
for a hundred miles through the desert, repenting.
You only have to let the soft animal of your body
love what it loves.'

Pagans don't usually talk about 'converting' to Paganism but, rather, about 'coming home'. They tend to recognize that the term 'Paganism' fits their spirituality, world view and lifestyle. It names the feelings and beliefs that they have held for a while. Some talk about having always had a kinship with animals or plants, or an interest in herbs that might aid healing, or a gift for doing magic. They have often hidden these passions and desires, not knowing that others shared them, fearing they might appear childish or foolish.

Networks and websites set out some minimum definitions, although in fact, without an official creed or authoritative hierarchy, anyone can call themselves a Pagan. Some say that a Pagan must venerate nature, acknowledge both female and male divinities or aspects of the divine, and affirm their commitment to living responsibly. One of the most influential networks is the British Pagan Federation, which provides information and contacts for Pagans and reliable information to the media and other interested groups. Its constitution enshrines three principles which, taken together, read like a core statement of belief, but the Federation accepts that 'not all Pagans feel able to agree with each or all of the Principles [and the Federation] still campaigns and supports ALL Pagans whether or not they can agree to the Principles.' The three principles are:

1. Love for and Kinship with Nature. Reverence for the life force and its ever-renewing cycles of life and death.
2. A positive morality, in which the individual is responsible for the discovery and development of their true nature in harmony with the outer world and community. This is often expressed as 'Do what you will, as long as it harms none.'
3. Recognition of the Divine, which transcends gender, acknowledging both the female and male aspect of Deity.[2]

These principles are inclusive, and allow for a wide range of interpretation. The first promotes a respect for nature and reminds us that humans are part of the community of life rather than beings who transcend its cycles of life and death. The second stresses ethical responsibility, and encourages the individual to be true to his or her potential, and respect others. The third points out that divinity is without gender (and, by implication, other potentially divisive characteristics such as ethnicity, class or age) but may be experienced in both male and female forms and expressions.

Many Pagans reject the Pagan Federation's particular understanding of deity, ethics and even nature. Some are radically polytheistic, insisting that many deities exist. Others are more animistic, believing that it is a mistake to give priority to deities and preferring to honour the whole community of living beings. However, there is little animosity or sectarian conflict even among those Pagans who question the need for anything that looks like a creed. Some outsiders find the diversity of Paganism bewildering, but most Pagans positively celebrate it, believing it to be as natural as the diversity of tree species in a healthy wood.

Paganism encompasses Druids, Goddess-feminists, Heathens, Witches or Wiccans, and various ethnic Pagans (those defining themselves in relation to a particular ancestry, e.g. Celtic, Greek or Lithuanian). There are Pagans who call themselves 'eclectic' and draw on any available source for their beliefs and practices. There are also particular subgroups within the larger Pagan strands: Druid Orders, ethnic Pagan Associations, Heathen Hearths and Wiccan covens. Estimates of the total numbers of Pagans vary wildly. The generally respected website 'adherents.com' offers a global total of one million and a US total of around 760,000.[3] More sceptical estimates of around a quarter of those figures have been proposed. Observers agree that it is not possible to give definitive numbers because there are no agreed rules for deciding who to include or exclude, and because Pagans may join many groups at once, or none at all. However, every indicator (membership of groups, readership of publications, hits on websites, participation in events) suggests that Paganism is growing numerically.

Among the more organized kinds of Paganism, sometimes called 'paths' or 'traditions', there are significant variations. Heathens and the ethnic Pagans draw on their respective ancestral literatures, archaeology and folklore in their worship. Some Druids do the same, but they also have much in common with Witches, who stress an initiatory ritual process that teaches self-knowledge along with methods of celebrating nature; Goddess-feminists stress feminist activism; eco-Pagans stress environmental activism; and shamanic Pagans (many of whom join Druid, Heathen, Wiccan or Goddess-centred groups) are particularly concerned with altering states of consciousness or awareness. The deities of these groups vary: Heathens venerate Anglo-Saxon, Norse, Icelandic and Germanic deities; Druids tend to honour the goddesses and gods mentioned in ancient British, Irish and Gallic temple inscriptions and in more recent Celtic literature and folklore; Witches invoke 'the Goddess and the God'; and Goddess-feminists revere 'the Goddess', even though she might have many names.

There are many ways to join a Pagan group. Anyone can participate in open events like festivals or pub meetings. Groups such as Wiccan covens have an introduction process, mutual testing, and an initiation ceremony that recognizes full membership. Wiccan initiation is similar to conversion in Judaism where you can think of yourself as Jewish but it is up to the community to recognize you and welcome you as a full member. Some Pagans prefer not to belong to organized groups, and call themselves 'solitaries'; but most are happy to meet with others to celebrate festivals and to gain new knowledge from fellow practitioners.

Not surprisingly, particular aspects of Paganism appeal to different groups of people. The focus on nature attracts those who want their spiritual life to address their concern for ecology or enhance their delight in rural or wilderness retreats. The stress on female deities in many Pagan traditions is attractive to feminists and all those who seek more inclusive groups. Women are also drawn to a religion in which they can take on significant leadership responsibilities and find powerful female role models. Young people are attracted by the promise that by doing magic they can play an important role in the world. In fact, many people are drawn to Pagan beliefs in magic. Although environmental activism is an appropriate response to some contemporary problems, the powerful symbolic actions of magic can bring about changes both in oneself and one's surroundings.

Most Pagans insist that celebrating nature, performing magic and honouring deities makes the world a better place for all their neighbours, not just the human ones but also the animals, plants and all other life. This reverence for life in all its forms is a common theme among many indigenous peoples and adds some weight to Pagan claims to be reviving or reconstructing the religious traditions of pre-Christian Europe. It is not that the details of ceremonial performance are identical, but that they share an underlying engagement with an inter-connected and inter-related world.

Like Aboriginal initiations, Pagan gatherings do not require the construction of permanent, purpose-built religious buildings. They can take place anywhere and everywhere: out in the countryside, in the wilderness, bush or parks, or inside people's homes, in pubs, hired meeting halls, or any other useful environment. During ceremonies Pagans create temporary ritual spaces, whose boundaries are marked with symbolic objects. Because all the earth is sacred there is nowhere that cannot host a Pagan gathering.

There is another sense in which Paganism is not confined: its influence and impact has spread into many media. Paganism is a popular topic of television and radio broadcasts, newspaper and magazine articles, and websites. Academics in various disciplines (Religious Studies, Sociology, Anthropology, Psychology and History) study Paganism and write books and articles about it, and any worthwhile introductory book or course about religions today will include something about it. 'Pagan' is no longer simply a pejorative term used and defined by Paganism's opponents. Paganism is growing in popularity not only among those who find it a satisfying way of experiencing and celebrating the sacred dimensions of the world but also among those interested in contemporary society.

2

Pagans today

Pagans are mostly concentrated in the countries of Europe, North America, South Africa, Australia and New Zealand, but it is not possible to say precisely how many Pagans there are in the world, as they do not all belong to one organization, or indeed, any organization. Pagans do not all identify themselves on national census returns, or they prefer labels like 'animist' that make it difficult to reach a final total. According to data presented by the UK Office for National Statistics, in the 2001 national census 31,000 people in England and Wales identified themselves as Pagans and a further 7,000 identified themselves as Wiccans. Those who wrote 'Heathen' in the space provided were included among those alleged to have 'no religion'.[4] Similar responses to censuses in Australia, Canada and New Zealand demonstrate the inadequacy of either the census questions or of their interpretation.[5]

Whatever the reliability of the censuses, the consensus among academics is towards continuing numerical growth.

Claims that Paganism is the fastest growing religion in the world are countered by similar claims made by a remarkable number of other religions or their branches, such as Pentecostal Christianity in many African countries, but certainly Paganism is gaining adherents. Festivals and conferences are well attended. Membership of umbrella organizations that link individual Pagans and small groups into larger networks show signs of growth.

Michael York, a sociologist of religion, has examined statistical surveys of the world's population and argues that Paganism is a member of a larger group of 'nature religions'. He uses the lower-case 'paganism' as an umbrella term under which he includes Chinese folk religion, Shinto, indigenous religions, spiritism and shamanism, as well as Paganism. He does not mean that all these religions are identical, but argues that they are distinct from other groups of religions because they 'furnish frameworks and techniques for encouraging experiential encounters with the godhead for both improving one's welfare in this world and exploring the otherworld in search of spiritual reward'.[6] All together these religions form nearly 6 per cent of the world's population. Self-identified Pagans (Druids, Heathens, Witches and so on) may be a small minority of the American or European population, but they are members of a much larger group of religions found throughout the world.

THE WORLD'S RELIGIOUS POPULATION

Christian/Islamic	50%
nonreligious/atheist	21%
Hindu-Buddhist	19%
pagan	5–6%
new religions	2%
other	1%

Source: Michael York, *Pagan Theology: Paganism as a World Religion* (2003). Among 'other', York includes Jews, Sikhs, Jains, Baha'is and various esotericists and Gnostics.

The majority of Pagans are white Europeans or of European ancestry. A recent survey of North American Pagans found that just over 90 per cent identified themselves as white.[7] A further 5 per cent refused to identify their ethnicity, 0.9 per cent were Native American, 0.2 per cent Asian, and less than 0.1 per cent either African American or Hispanic. Despite the prominence the surveys gives it, ethnic identity is not of great significance in Paganism. Indeed, recent decades have seen the revitalization of many indigenous religious cultures so that many Native Americans, Aboriginal Australians, Africans and Pacific Islanders participate in traditional ceremonies that honour the earth and life in ways that are comparable to Pagan practices.

While Paganism has no ethnic characteristics or requirements built into its principles, as in many religions there are a handful of groups which do lay considerable stress on the alleged superiority of their particular ethnicity (whether this is, for example, Anglo-Saxon, Celtic or Slavic). Such groups are often not only racist, claiming that there is some kind of 'natural' link between alleged types of people and types of religion, but also homophobic and misogynist. In their hands, words like 'nature' or 'natural' not only to refer to, for example, organic foods but also to suspect ideas about the 'purity of the race' and the superiority of particular ways of life. The majority of Pagans find such views dubious and disreputable, and argue that the very notion of race is of recent origin and jars with the broader Pagan world view which celebrates the diversity of life. Since the groups that espouse such ideas are quite small, Pagans rarely devote much energy or time to debate these issues.

Pagans are, though, concerned with the question of group structure and related power dynamics. Paganism is made up of a large number of groups of widely differing shapes and sizes: solitary individuals, tight-knit localized groups, national and international networks. There is no central organization to which all Pagans belong, no single magazine that all Pagans read, no religious leader who unites all groups. Some Pagans belong to several different groups simultaneously. There are Heathens who celebrate festivals organized by Druids. Many members of Wiccan covens also identify themselves as Shamans and/or as Goddess-feminists.

Sociologists have argued about how best to describe Paganism's structure. Michael York has described it as a SPIN: a 'Segmented Polycentric Integrated Network'.[8] Like the World Wide Web it links innumerable individuals via a host of providers which offer particular kinds of service.

The American author and activist known as Starhawk is one of the most thoughtful writers on Pagan authority structures or power dynamics. In *Dreaming the Dark* (1982) she contrasted 'power-over' with 'power-from-within', and promoted a third kind of power: 'power-with'. 'Power-over' is the kind of domineering and controlling power at the heart of patriarchy: the cultural system that privileges male authority over everyone and everything else. 'Power-from-within' is more akin to 'ability' and recognizes that everyone has a contribution to make in the world. 'Power-with', as identified by Starhawk and other feminist writers like Carol Christ, is a fully participative and consensus-seeking democracy. Many Pagan groups and meetings are organized without leaders but with facilitators or enablers. Sometimes decision-making positions are rotated throughout the group so that no single individual gains dominance. Even in Pagan groups with clergy (usually called priestesses and priests) celebrations are conducted in circles rather than rows or lines, and everyone is encouraged to participate. The offering of invocations to deities, ancestors and helpful other-than-human persons (especially elemental beings – earth, air, fire and water – but also trees and maybe the faery folk) is rarely performed by a solitary leader. Everyone is a participant; there are no observers. Just as all living beings (deities, humans, hedgehogs, herons, salmon, bees, oaks and the rest) participate in making the world what it is, so Pagan activities that celebrate life are all about participation.

Some Witches and Goddess-feminists claim that they venerate the same Great Goddess as the Palaeolithic ancestors who carved female figures into the entrances of the caves they decorated with rock-art, or the Neolithic ancestors who left female statuettes in their temples and homes. Some Druids claim that they practise similar seasonal ceremonies as the Iron Age British or Irish Celts. A few Wiccans believe they perform magical rituals identical to those of the persecuted witches of medieval and early modern Europe. Yet most Heathens and many other Pagans are careful to explain that their religion is a not a revival but a reconstruction relevant to today, from sources like the Sagas and Eddas which provide the outlines of practices common among their ancestors before Christianity. Most happily create new activities out of their creative imagination and experimentation. Clearly there can be radically different answers to the question of when Paganism started.

Although many people have been accused of Paganism throughout the centuries – of not belonging to the monotheistic religions or of opposing Christianity – only in the middle of the twentieth century did significant numbers identify themselves, their beliefs and practices with Pagan religion. Paganism was not started by one person, group or event, but there are plenty of founders of particular Pagan groups, and events that could be pointed to as the origin of particular branches. Gerald Gardner founded Wicca; Ross Nichols and some American college students created new ways to be Druids; Zsuzsanna Budapest and Starhawk established feminist versions of Paganism.

Every Pagan knows something about Gerald Gardner. According to some he created the new Pagan way of being a 'Witch' or 'Wiccan', although others believe that he made better known an existing witchcraft tradition. In 1951, following the repeal of the Witchcraft and Vagrancy Acts (when it ceased to be a criminal offence in the UK to claim to be a witch), Gerald Gardner, a retired civil servant, wrote *Witchcraft Today*,[9] in which he described a coven of Witches he claimed to have joined in the 1940s to work magic and honour the 'old Gods' secretly in 'natural', rural environments in southern England. He described how an ancient Pagan fertility religion had gone underground for many centuries to survive the Christian persecution of 'witches', but was now becoming public again. The idea and the practice soon came to be called 'Wicca' (from an Anglo-Saxon word meaning 'witch' but also understood by many Pagans to mean 'wise', or associated with 'bending' as in the crafts of hedge-laying or working magic to reshape the way things are). Gardner and friends initiated others, first as members of their coven and later as 'High Priestesses' and 'High Priests', those with the right to set up daughter covens. A

lineage began. Or, if Gardner is to be believed, an ancient
lineage gained many new branches and members. Either
way, Wiccan High Priestesses aided by their High Priests
now initiate new priestesses and priests, as each full member
of a coven is known, and teach them the seasonal and
magical rituals of the Craft (as Wicca is also called).

Gardner's story of an ancient, hidden fertility religion
was an inspiring manifesto to many people in the early days
of the Pagan revival. It was inherited from what seemed
like reputable academic sources, such as the 1929 article on
'Witchcraft' by the Egyptologist Margaret Murray printed
in various editions of the *Encyclopedia Britannica*.[10]
Gardner and his friends presented Wicca as a natural exten-
sion of an earlier religion, for those with 'an attraction for
the occult, a sense of wonder, a feeling that you can slip for
a few minutes out of this world into the other world of
faery'.[11] Ronald Hutton, author of *The Triumph of the
Moon: A History of Modern Pagan Witchcraft* (1999), and
other historians have shown that the real history of witchcraft was rather different than what Murray had proposed;
witchcraft was an accusation made against innocents that
led to widespread persecution. Most Pagans now accept
that Gardner created a new religion by blending ideas drawn
from folk stories and other interests, including amateur
anthropology, naturism and esotericism, with the esoteric
rituals of groups like the Freemasons, updating them for his
time with a strong stress on communion with the natural
world.

The Wiccan movement did not entirely follow Murray's theology or sociology. She claimed that the 'Witch Cult' worshipped a single male deity in covens led by high priests, whereas the new Witches venerated a goddess and a god in covens led by pairs of high priestesses and high priests working together. This increased stress on a goddess or even goddesses was due to the influence on the first Wiccans by books like Robert Graves's *The White Goddess* (1948), which argued that ancient pagans in Greece, Rome and Ireland venerated a single great goddess.

Many of the initiation rites and magical rituals in Wicca bear similarities to those of groups like the Order of the Golden Dawn and the Freemasons – especially the Co-Masons, a movement in which women participated alongside men. These were esoteric movements which followed ceremonial rituals to gain self-knowledge and self-empowerment. Like them, Wiccans conduct their ceremonies in circles consecrated with symbolic implements (e.g. a dagger), and purified with salt and water. They greet the four quarters (east, south, west and north) and the elements (air, fire, water and earth) associated with them. The poet and playwright W. B. Yeats, a member of the Order of the Golden Dawn, wrote poetry that blended Irish mythology and folklore with esoteric teachings and Christian themes. Although he remained a Christian, he contributed to a broad cultural movement that spoke respectfully of the Dagda, Dana, Angus and Sidhe, pre-Christian Irish deities, heroes and otherworld beings encountered in rural and ancient landscapes. Aleister Crowley, another Golden Dawn member, had even greater influence on Gardner. He suggested communing with the old, pagan deities, and celebrating what D. H. Lawrence called 'pagan desires', for the good for the world.[12] Maybe Crowley meant no more than that ancient stories and ceremonies would enliven rituals that promoted self-knowledge and personal growth. Gerald Gardner and his friends transformed the Golden Dawn rituals, rooting them in the celebration of nature and the veneration of a deity who was believed to be an actual being, the Goddess, rather than merely a powerful metaphor. This new relationship with a deity also involved a shift away from an individualistic and inward-looking idea of the 'self' towards a more relational notion: Wiccan magical ceremonies inculcate the understanding that the true self exists in relationship with deities, other humans, all living beings, and the earth itself.

'The Charge of the Goddess' by Doreen Valiente revises an initiatory speech which Gerald Gardner derived from the rituals and writings of various magical groups, especially Charles Leland's *Aradia* and Aleister Crowley's *Book of the Law*.[13] In most Witchcraft traditions a version of this 'Charge' is recited by the presiding priestess, considered a manifestation of the Goddess during ceremonies:

'Whenever ye have need of anything, once in the month, and better it be when the Moon is full, then shall ye assemble in some secret place and adore the spirit of me, who am Queen of all Witcheries. There shall ye assemble, ye who are fain to learn all sorcery, yet have not won its deepest secrets; to these will I teach things that are yet unknown. And ye shall be free from slavery, and as a sign that ye be really free ye shall be naked in your rites and ye shall dance, sing, feast, make music and love, all in my praise. For mine is the ecstasy of the spirit, and mine also is joy on Earth, for my law is love unto all beings. Keep pure your highest ideal, strive ever towards it; let nought stop you or turn you aside. For mine is the secret door which opens upon the land of youth and mine is the cup of the wine of life and the Cauldron of Ceridwen, which is the Holy Grail of Immortality. I am the gracious Goddess who gives the gift of joy unto the heart of man; upon Earth I give knowledge of the Spirit eternal, and beyond death I give peace and freedom and reunion with those who have gone before. Nor do I demand sacrifice, for behold I am the Mother of all living, and my love is poured out upon the Earth.'

The emphasis on relationships encouraged Wiccans to open membership more widely, and increasingly to celebrate with other Pagans. The democratization of witchcraft took its most dramatic turn in the 1970s when feminist Pagans questioned the inherited power dynamics. Zsuzsanna Budapest in the USA questioned why a priestess needed the company of a priest to perform ceremonies or magic and why goddesses needed to be accompanied by gods. Feminist Goddess-spirituality increased the appeal of Pagan groups, and led some to join women-only groups such as Dianic covens (distinguished from other covens by their women-only membership and their exclusive devotion to female deities).

Starhawk not only stressed the importance of the Goddess (or goddesses) and women, but also demonstrated, with other feminists, the value of magical rituals in activist events that try to change situations that damage, threaten or diminish the lives of people and the world around them. Activist Pagans belong to groups that include, among others, the Reclaiming network, Earth First!, the Dongas, Dragon Environmental Network, and the Matriarchy Study Group. At the Greenham Common women's peace camps protesting a cruise missile base in Britain between 1981 and 2000, the rituals of protest, including weaving wool into the fence and hanging pentagrams on the gates to oppose war, were inspirational to Pagans and encouraged the Pagan trend towards radical activism.

Other kinds of Paganism were developing alongside Gardner's Wicca. New groups of Pagan Druids drew inspiration from Iron Age and 'Celtic' pagan traditions, filtered through Roman, medieval and more recent writings. A composite picture from these sources shows ancient Druids as political, cultural and ritual leaders. They could be respected as philosophers but were also vilified as political and religious opponents by both Romans and Christians. Archaeological evidence shows that Iron Age British, Gaulish and Irish religion was polytheistic and centred around many local deities and shrines, possibly with a few more national deities (such as a solar deity named Lugh, Llew or Lug). Iron Age Druids could be compared with the elite Brahmin caste in Hinduism, who facilitate public rituals in present-day villages in India and are traditionally the spiritual leaders and philosophers of the nation.

THE DRUIDS IN CLASSICAL AND MEDIEVAL LITERATURE[14]

Julius Caesar (100–44 BCE, Roman emperor): 'They preside over sacred things, have the change of public and private sacrifices, and explain their religion.'

Diodorus Siculus (90–21 BCE, Greek historian): 'The Pythagorean doctrine prevails among them, teaching that the souls of men are immortal and live again for a fixed number of years inhabited in another body.'

Strabo (63 BCE–24 CE, Greek geographer and historian): 'Among them there are generally three classes to whom special honour is paid: the Bards, the Vatis, and the Druids ... The Druids studied nature and moral philosophy.'

Pliny the Elder (23–79 CE; Roman encyclopedist): 'The Druids, as they call their magicians, consider nothing more sacred than mistletoe and the tree on which it grows, provided that it is an oak. They ... perform no sacred rites with oak leaves. It is from this custom that they seem to have been called Druids, based on the Greek interpretation of that word [i.e. Greek *drys*, oak].'

Diogenes Laertius (3rd century CE, Greek philosopher): 'The Druids make their pronouncements by means of riddles and dark sayings, teaching that the gods must be worshipped, and no evil done, and manly behaviour maintained.'

St John Chrysostom (c. 374–407CE, Christian patriarch of Constantinople): '... Druids, who concern themselves with divination and all branches of wisdom.'

Book of Hui Maine (11th century CE, medieval Irish text): 'A wage was given to [the Druid] Mog Ruith who chose it for beheading John [the Baptist]; this then was the wage of Mog Ruith, [his] choice of the maidens. Then Mog Ruith the splendid went to kill John, though it was shameful. So he took in the prison to Herod the head of John on a dish of white silver.'

Between the Iron Age and the mid-twentieth century various groups have claimed to be Druids. The majority of later Druids were not polytheistic Pagans, but Christians for whom 'Druid' meant philosopher, holder of tradition, and pillar of society: they usually imagined their Celtic predecessors as noble teachers of profound wisdom. Most Druid groups were charitable organizations or 'friendly societies', associations that offered help to members and their families in difficult times. Like similar groups such as the Royal Foresters, they performed ceremonies that were intended to be evocative and unifying rather than religiously meaningful. Some added the maintenance of local culture to their purposes. In the 1790s Iolo Morganwg collected and wrote Druidic texts and liturgies to strengthen Welsh culture and language, developing ceremonies that could be conducted in new and ancient stone circles, but he was also a regular participant in his local Nonconformist chapel. Over the next century and a half the majority of Druid Orders blended esotericism, mutual support and charity. In Brittany, however, the Druid revival of the eighteenth century mixed a polytheistic veneration of Iron Age deities with an attempt to maintain a distinctive Breton language and culture. As among many indigenous people today, the celebration of local languages is a powerfully effective way of maintaining traditional life, rituals and beliefs.

Iolo Morganwg wrote a prayer that is still used by many
Druids today. Some continue to use the original,
Nonconformist Christian language, others address the
prayer to a goddess, polytheistic deities or to 'Spirit'. In its
'Goddess' form the prayer reads:

'Grant O Goddess, your protection
and in protection, strength
and in strength, understanding
and in understanding, knowledge
and in knowledge, the knowledge of justice
and in the knowledge of justice, the love of it
and in the love of it, the love of all existences
and in the love of all existences, the love of Goddess and
all Goodness.'

In 1963 a group of students invented the 'Reformed
Druids of North America' (RDNA) to test a rule at
Carleton College, Northfield, Minnesota, that they must all
attend church services. They convinced the authorities that
RDNA was a legitimate religion and having won their
case – which exempted them from attending Christian
churches – many found that the ceremonies they invented
were deeply satisfying. Initially these involved a summer
and winter ritual in which a tree branch was offered to the
'Earth-mother' and participants shared the 'waters of life'

(whisky) or the 'waters of sleep' (water). More elaborate ceremonies involving the celebration of other seasonal festivals and the consecration of all participants evolved. When they graduated from the college some continued to call themselves Druids. Their tradition evolved, especially in a branch called the New Reformed Druids of North America (NRDNA).

In England, Ross Nichols left the Ancient Druid Order, a Masonic-style esoteric movement, to establish the Order of Bards, Ovates and Druids (OBOD) in 1963. Nichols's OBOD blended a quest for self-knowledge with a celebration of seasonal cycles, nature, and a delight in Celtic literature and myths. OBOD is open to people of any religion or none, but many Pagan members value its emphasis on the arts of musicianship, poetry and storytelling (the activity of 'bards'), healing (the activity of 'ovates'), and teaching (the activity of 'druids').[15] Most other Pagan Druid Orders encourage the same range of arts, finding evidence of their importance in ancient and historical references to Celtic religions, but few follow OBOD's separation of Bards, Ovates and Druids into three hierarchical grades.

While some Druid Orders have established national or international networks, others root themselves firmly in particular places. The Secular Order, for example, celebrates being a West Country (of England) Order with particular focus on the area around and between Stonehenge and Bath.[16] It has reinvigorated the tradition of annual competitive bardic events like those of the Welsh, Cornish and

Breton *Eisteddfodau* (performance events) by encouraging
all kinds of popular music, poetry and performance.

Reconstructions of the religions of pre-Christian Iceland,
Scandinavia and Anglo-Saxon Britain are also of growing
significance among contemporary Pagans. Heathens (as
most practitioners prefer to be called) draw on ancient
literature like the anonymous thirteenth-century *Saga
of Eirik the Red* and the *Havamal*,[17] as well as archaeology,
anthropology, folklore, imagination, experience and experimentation to develop new ways of practising their religion.
Not only do they revere ancestral deities like Odin, Thor,
Freya and Sif, but are inspired by stories of the nine realms
of the universe linked by the Yggdrasil, the tree that forms
the axis around which the world and the cosmos turn,
and by 'wyrd', a web of life and fate that links everyone and
everything.

One of the most interesting developments among
Heathens is the revival of shamanic practices, such as seeking knowledge while in trance, altered awareness and
consciousness, and ways of communicating with powerful
beings such as deities and spirits of the land. While most
neo-shamans believe shamanism to be a set of techniques
of use for therapeutic and self-improvement purposes
(based on the works of Carlos Castaneda, Mircea Eliade
and Michael Harner), Heathen shamans root their
shamanic work in an animistic understanding of the
world as a community of living beings, only some of whom
are human.[18] Their shamanism is more like a conversation

with helpful beings such as animals, plants, rocks, ancestors, deities and land-wights (spirits of places) than an exploration of inner realities. While the Sagas and other ancient sources indicate that ancestral Heathens practiced shamanry, entering a trance state and calling on the deities to aid healing, they do not detail the precise techniques by which consciousness is altered or other-than-human beings are communicated with. Instead they lay considerable stress on the costume and equipment of practitioners and only hint at elements of their performance.

The following extract from *The Saga of Eirik the Red* describes the visit of a seeress (*spákona* or *völva*) named þorbjörg (Thorbjörg) to a farm in Greenland around a thousand years ago:[19]

'At that time [there] was a great famine in Greenland; those men who had gone on fishing expeditions caught little (and some did not return). That woman was there in the village, who was called þorbjörg; she was a prophetess and was called "little völva" [. . .] It was þorbjörg's habit during [the] winter that she went to feasts and those men welcomed her most at [their] home[s] who were eager to know their destiny or [that of the] season; and because þorkell was then the most powerful farmer it seemed his duty to find out when this bad season, which beset [them], might finish. þorkell invites the prophetess home, and she is given a good welcome, as the custom was, when a woman of this kind is received. The high seat was made ready for her and a cushion laid under her; there should be hens' feathers in[side it]. And when she came during the evening together with that man, who was sent to meet her, then was she so dressed, that she had over her a blue cloak with a strap, and [it] was set [with] stones all [over the] skirts; she had glass beads on her neck, a black lambskin kerchief (with white catskin inside) on her head; and she had a staff in [her] hand, and [there] was a knob on [it]; it was ornamented with brass and stones [were] set below the knob; she had a belt about her and a large skin purse was on it, and she preserved therein her charms, those which she needed to have [for her] magic. She had calfskin shoes on [her] feet, and long thongs on [them] and large tin knobs on the end [of them]. She had catskin gloves on her hands and [they] were white inside and hairy. And when she came in, it seemed to all people [that they] should accord her honourable greetings. [. . .] Women then formed a ring around the dais that þorbjörg sat upon. Guðríðr [a local woman who knew a chant called Varðlokur which is "necessary for the spell"] sang the song so fairly and [so] well that none there at that time thought [they had] heard the song sung by a fairer voice. The prophetess thanked her [for] the song and said

many of those spirits had now sought [them] and
considered [it] fair to listen [to], when the song was so
well sung – "who before wished to separate [themselves
from] us and never grant us obedience. But now many
[of] those things are apparent to me, which before were
hidden [from] me, and many others."'

þorbjörg goes on to answer the questions of the whole
community, beginning with the farmer's concern about the
famine.

While books about archaeology, history, anthropology,
folklore, ecology and herbalism inform Paganism, it is hard
to overestimate the importance of works of fiction and fantasy. Ideas in Robert Heinlein's *Stranger in a Strange Land*
inspired some American Pagans to create the Church of All
Worlds (CAW) network;[20] Marion Bradley's *Mists of Avalon*
has provided one model for understanding the nature of
the Goddess and the role of priestesses; Alan Garner's *The
Weirdstone of Brisingamen* has enchanted many Pagans while
reminding them of the importance of place, and his *The
Owl Service* sets a standard for the re-telling of ancient
legends; Brian Bates's *The Way of Wyrd* laid the foundations
for many Pagans' shamanic ideas; and Terry Pratchett's *Wyrd
Sisters*, and the rest of his comic fantasy Discworld series has
entertained many Pagans. These are just a few of the more well

known books. Pagans believe that we need to imagine new ways of living and this kind of literature encourages the hard work of making the world a better place. Paganism, like all new religions, draws from deep wells; and, like all old religions that are still alive, it can still teach youngsters how to dance.

3

Celebrating nature

All Pagan practices, such as festivals, magic and beliefs about deities, are wrapped up with the fundamental belief in the goodness of nature. Pagan conversations, stories, publications and websites focus on festivals that honour the changing seasons and the movements of the earth, sun, moon, planets and stars, the central and defining concerns of Pagans. Every Pagan celebrates festivals but they do so in distinct ways and at different times and places. Nature is both Paganism's common ground and the wellspring of its diversity.

A quick search for definitions of Paganism on the internet demonstrates the importance of nature. Even in definitions that add other things – such as magic or beliefs about deities – it is clear that nature is fundamental. For example, the UK's Pagan Federation

defines a Pagan as 'A follower of a polytheistic or
pantheistic nature-worshipping religion' and Paganism as
'A polytheistic or pantheistic nature-worshipping
religion.'[21]

Similarly, the FAQ section of the website of the Church
of All Worlds[22] says: 'Neo-Paganism is a revival and
reconstruction of ancient Nature religions adapted for the
modern world. It is a religion of the living Earth . . . Neo-
Paganism is a natural religion, viewing humanity as a
functional organ within the greater organism of all Life,
rather than as something special created separate and
"above" the rest of the natural world. Neo-Pagans seek
not to conquer Nature, but to harmonize and integrate
with Her. Neo-Paganism should be regarded as "Green
Religion", just as we have "Green Politics" and "Green
Economics".'

Every place is affected by changing seasons and climates.
In north-west Europe there are four seasons: spring,
summer, autumn and winter. In northern Australia there is
a wet and a dry season. Every location has its prevailing
winds, and its variations in the hours of expected sunlight
or rainfall. In some areas there are myriad springs of fresh
water that flow into rivers and eventually into oceans, in
other places the water table is so low that you have to dig
deep to quench your thirst. The soils that form different

landscapes can be vastly different from one another too: there are arid sands, silty loams and claggy clays. Beneath these or emerging through them can be igneous, sedimentary or metamorphic rocks, each layering the earth over millions of years of growth and change, forming vast plates that move slowly around the globe, and affecting the life supported on the relatively thin top layer of soil or water. Some places are inhabited by a vast diversity of plants, birds, animals, fish, insects and microbes, others are almost devoid of life.

Every place on earth is crossed by the sun, moon and stars as they travel across the sky. At least, it looks this way – even scientists seem to see the sun move from east to west each day. If you stand in one place every day for a year and mark the point on the eastern horizon where the sun rises you will see a pattern emerge. At the spring and autumn equinoxes (usually 21 March and 21 September, when the lengths of day and night are equal) the sun rises due east. In the northern hemisphere it rises further to the north each day until midsummer (around 21 June), when it appears to stop and then begin its journey southwards again. At midwinter (around 21 December) it reaches its most southerly rising point, stops and then heads north again. These standing and turning points are the solstices, meaning 'sun standstill'. The moon also rises in a different position each day or night, but traces a more complex pattern in a cycle that lasts over nineteen years between its most northerly and southerly standstills. We also see the moon growing from a thin crescent to full roundness and then shrinking to another crescent in a process that still defines a monthly cycle for many people.

The ancient temple of Stonehenge marks the cycles of the sun, moon, planets and stars in relation to the earth. Heading out from the centre of the circle, a processional avenue is bordered by outlying standing stones between which the midsummer sun rises. If you turn your back to that solstice alignment you then face the midwinter sunset position. The lunar standstills are also honoured, rising and setting within particular 'gateways' between the massive standing stones. Although there is considerable debate about the original uses of Stonehenge, it has been the site of midsummer celebrations for centuries. Stonehenge is a place of considerable sanctity not only for Druids (who some people think have been involved with the temple for millennia) but for all kinds of Pagans. Thousands gather at the solstices and other festivals.

Beneath the sun, moon and stars, on the earth's varying soils or in its waters, living beings are born or hatched, eat and are eaten, breed, sometimes grow to maturity, and die. Bodies of flesh and fibre rot down, returning nutrients into the earth in a complex cycle of life. And they do all this with relatives and friends, enemies and acquaintances. This blue-green planet that is our home houses a profligate abundance of life.

Every human and every living being, literally every *body*, shares in this braided story of the Earth's abundant life. For Pagans, all the ordinary, everyday, worldly, physical facts of life, such as birds singing and the changing length of days, are worthy of celebration. Sometimes they are the cause of joy, but since life includes death and disease they can also be the cause of sorrow and mourning. It is not that 'nice nature' (sunrise, spring, birth, sexuality) is a cause of joy while 'nasty nature' (long winter nights, death, disease, predation) is resisted. Pagans believe that every aspect of nature should be honoured, every part of the cycle of life and death, including those you don't necessarily like. So, in their winter festivals especially, most Pagans take time to honour the dead with offerings and greetings, and to consider the role of death in natural and cosmic lifecycles.

Our personal lives are also marked by something like seasons. Not only are we born, grow older and die, but we also feel more alive at some times and in some places than in others. Some people are happier by the seaside on a midsummer's day while others prefer wild storms on a winter's night. Pagans encourage the celebration of these individual seasons and personal preferences.

In the last sixty years Pagans have gradually accepted that cities are included in the saying '*all* the Earth is sacred'. 'Nature' is not elsewhere, away from the cities, and different to humanity. It is wherever you are. Today, some Pagans celebrate seasons in urban spaces rather than making pilgrimages into rural environments or wildernesses. Others try to make cities more ecological, bio-diverse, liveable and

organic. The Pagan group Reclaiming has been at the fore-
front of anti-globalization campaigns (especially when the
G8 leaders meet), protesting against the power of militarily
dominant governments, multinational companies and their
shareholders. These activist campaigns show the contours of
Paganism's radicalism.

Pagans use religious rather than everyday language to
express the belief that 'all the world is sacred' or, quoting
William Blake, 'Every thing that lives is Holy.'[23] They
might equally say, 'Earth is our home.' They are enchanted
by the magic of sunrises, fires, festive meals, and the conversation of living beings sharing the beauty of being alive.
These pleasures inspire Pagans to improve the world and to
address significant problems generated by different ways of
seeing the Earth, especially the idea that everything (trees,
minerals, animals, water) is a resource to be bought and
sold. Pagan motivations are in stark contrast to the motivations of someone who wants to go to 'heaven', to escape
from ordinary mortal life and become 'enlightened', or
who doesn't really notice the world, thinking it is just the
scenery in which the real action, human life, takes place.
Even the scientific recognition that the earth moves around
the sun can deny our everyday sense that the sun moves
across the sky. We fit the world in every way: the world is
full of bird songs and we have ears, it has rainbows and we
have eyes, it has flowers and we have noses, it has stones
and we have fingers, it has figs and we have tongues. We
are watery and need to drink, we are physical and respond

to gravity. Our senses place us in relation to a wonderfully alive and varied world.[24] Human lives are braided into everything and everyone (human and other-than-human) around us. Pagans believe that this is a great gift worth celebrating.

A Pagan chant draws attention to the links and similarities between our bodies and that of the world. It involves the four elements – earth, wind, fire and water – which Greek philosophy and the European esoteric traditions considered the constituents of all things. It speaks eloquently of the earthiness of our bodies, the aliveness of the world, and the fit between the two:

'Earth's my body,
Water's my blood,
Air's my breath,
And fire's my spirit.'

Many humans think they are superior to other living beings, and that 'nature' is far removed from 'culture': the first is scenery, the second is what we humans do. Many, especially since the European Enlightenment in the eighteenth century, proclaim that they are fully conscious in a way no other animal is, let alone any other kind of living being, although some grudgingly accept that dolphins and gorillas may be self-conscious too. Not dogs or bats or budgerigars, however, and certainly not mosquitoes or gum trees. This hierarchy spells pain and death for many animals and plants, and provides another focus for Pagan activism.

Paganism's response to the arrogant actions that result from these false beliefs – especially the mass killing of many species and the eradication of diverse living places, ecologies or homes – is not utopian. 'Utopia' literally means 'no place'; it is imagined as being elsewhere, somewhere unknown or impossible to reach. Pagan solutions to the consequences of human arrogance are neither fantastic nor do they require that we move elsewhere. They celebrate places, and seek ways to belong wherever they are and to be intimate with all beings who live with them. They honour the senses and the sensual world, trying to live gently, without harm, in the world. Paganism blends ecologically respectful living with celebratory ceremonies rooted in the notion that the earth is the only home of humanity and of the whole host of living species, all of which deserve respect. The term 'eutopia', from the Greek words for 'good' and 'place', has been used to describe this Pagan celebration of belonging.

Pagan beliefs require not only that we protect threatened ecosystems, but that we replace the human domination of the world with respectful, neighbourly living alongside all other life. We must stop treating the world as if it were given to us, as if we have the right to control everything, or as if we aren't a part of it. This radical change begins with simple steps: celebrating the seasons, climates, ecological diversity, geographic and geological features of the place where you live. It begins with enjoying the songs sung by the birds who live near you, appreciating the colours of the butterflies who share your environment, honouring the sleek health of the badgers who are your neighbours. This need not degenerate into fluffy romanticism: birds, caterpillars and insects will eat the plants you are growing, and the badgers will dig holes in what you think is your garden. It is not that you have to let them, but that your efforts to stop them cannot involve the total war that results in ecocide: the extinction of life that results, say, from the agricultural industry's reliance on 'pesticides'. Everyone has problems with their neighbours and everyone has to find a way to live alongside them.

Pagan groups have developed cycles of seasonal festivals in which all of these beliefs, commitments and passions are celebrated and examined. Most Pagans follow a pattern of eight annual festivals that blend Celtic and Anglo-Saxon celebrations into a powerful way of marking the year. This works best in north-west Europe but has been adapted by Pagans in the southern hemisphere and in places with two rather than four annual seasons. The summer and winter solstices along with the spring and autumn equinoxes form four spokes of the wheel of the year, marking the middle of the four seasons. Four other festivals – usually given Irish or Anglo-Saxon names – mark the beginnings and ends of the seasons. The festival of Samhain (pronounced 'sow-ain') coincides in date and purpose with the Christian festival of Halloween, All Hallows, and All Souls: it honours the dead, pays respect to powerful beings, and permits the contemplation of mortality. Falling at the beginning of winter (1 November) it has been proposed as a special Pagan New Year. After winter, the festival of Imbolc (1 February) honours the coming of spring, made visible in the birth of the first lambs and the flowering of snowdrops. Summer begins with Beltain (1 May), a festival of love and passion anticipating increasing vitality throughout the summer. Lughnasad (1 August) takes its name from the celebration of the birth of the talented Irish deity, Lugh, who is associated with sunlight, ripening corn and prowess. The festival is also named Lammas, following Saxon Christian tradition, meaning 'Loaf Mass', and celebrates the beginning of the grain harvest. Each of these festivals is an occasion for gatherings to celebrate nature as well as contemplate the resonance of the season or time of year in our personal lives. At harvest times Pagans consider what they have achieved in a year. At Samhain, while honouring the dead, they acknowledge their failings, and commit themselves to try again. At winter solstice, as the sun begins to travel northwards along the horizon, bringing summer back again, Pagans contemplate their hopes for the coming year.

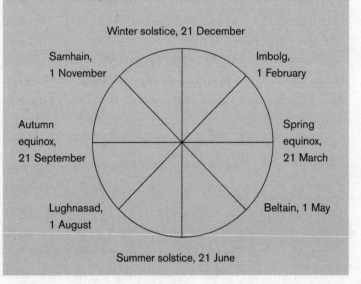

THE 'WHEEL OF THE YEAR': the most popular cycle of Pagan calendar festivals and their approximate dates in the northern hemisphere

Winter solstice, 21 December

Samhain, 1 November

Imbolg, 1 February

Autumn equinox, 21 September

Spring equinox, 21 March

Lughnasad, 1 August

Beltain, 1 May

Summer solstice, 21 June

4

Working magic

Magic is the distinctive activity of Pagan Witches and, even if it is not the defining characteristic of all kinds of Paganism, most Pagans practise it sometimes. One of the main reasons Pagans gather together in groups is to work magic. Thousands of teenagers read Pagan books, call themselves Pagans, and make contact with other Pagans locally or on the internet because of their interest in magic. This magic can be effective and satisfying, but sometimes complex and frustrating. Although magic is at the heart of Paganism, it is difficult to say that Pagans *believe* in it because, although many Pagans do magic or perform magical rituals, they do not necessarily believe that magic always works.

Magic is often lampooned, usually by those who know little about those who practise it, how it works, how its successes and failures can be explained, and how it relates to religion or science. Apart from those Christians who associate magic with their devil, this denigration is a hangover from when magic was considered a primitive phase of human cultural evolution. According to this prejudice, a primitive belief in magic was followed by the growth of religions and then, quite recently, by progress towards proper scientific experimentation and rationality. In this context, saying that you work magic is like admitting to superstition.

Some consider magic to be an attempt to control forces or beings beyond themselves, while religion honours or worships such forces or beings. The implication is that magic demonstrates a false sense of one's self-importance. Others have claimed that 'religious' people are weak-willed and subservient compared to 'magicians' who are strong, capable people dealing with the powers of the cosmos as equals or at least as responsible partners. Neither polemic represents the more balanced Pagan understanding, where those who practise magic believe there are limits to its use and practise it respectfully.

Two definitions of magic are current among Pagans: some say that magic is the art of causing change according to will, others that magic is the art of changing consciousness according to will. The first asserts that magic can change the world; it can heal a sick relative or make someone fall in love. The second suggests that magic can change one's self at the deep level of one's consciousness. This second definition is more fundamental to Pagan belief. Magic helps people know themselves better, understand reality more fully, and improve their ability to live more fully in the world around them. Both forms of magic grow from noble roots: one from the long tradition of pragmatism, the other from the equally long and equally profound tradition of esotericism. The first can be a means of getting what you or your family and friends need or want; the second as an attempt to become what you want to be.

Digging a little deeper it becomes clear that the two are much the same. The definitions of both pragmatic magic (getting what you want) and esoteric magic (becoming what you want to be) include the idea that changes are effected 'according to will'. This 'will' is not just your intentions for a particular ceremony, but refers to your true self, the real you at its best. It includes your understanding, knowledge and highest standards, your vision of how things could be at their best for everyone.

If magic is the art of changing consciousness according to will, it involves attempting to be the person you really want to be, the best you can be, the wisest, the most aware, the most helpful. Both Pagans and esotericists have described it as the encouragement of the 'higher self', 'divine self' or 'true self' within each person. It begins with the ancient injunction to 'know yourself', and it continues as a quest to know yourself better, and to empower yourself to live up to your own highest standards. If magic is the art of causing change according to will, it involves the same process: self-knowledge, self-empowerment and self-realization. If you can achieve this, it is obvious that 'getting what you want' is not about changing the world solely for your pleasure. Magic can be abused for selfish or self-aggrandizing ends, but built into the main definitions of magic are encouragements to be a better person.

One of the most commonly quoted summaries of Pagan ethics, especially when it comes to the working of magic, is a phrase originating among Wiccans: 'Do what ye will and ye harm none.' In translation from its archaic form this Wiccan Rede (or counsel), as it is called, advises that 'If it harm none, do as you will.' Of course, it may be as difficult to be sure that you won't harm anyone as it is to know your true will in the first place.

The Wiccan Rede adds a significant note to Aleister Crowley's 'Law of Thelema': 'Do what you will shall be the whole of the Law.' But even Crowley insisted that 'love is the law, love under will'. And both the Rede and the Law originate in the Christian Saint Augustine's instruction, 'Love and do what you will.'

Wiccans also quote a 'law of threefold return', saying that any magic will affect the magic worker three times more than they intend it to affect others. This is rarely meant to be understood literally, instead it serves as a caution to think before you act. It is most often used when practitioners instruct others not to try to harm others by magical curses.

In modern life we are often made to feel powerless and alone. Whichever way we vote, it seems unlikely that the people in power will do what we think they should. We can spend our lives working at jobs making things that we can't afford to take home. Some of us can't even afford our own homes. Television presents us with images that few can live up to. Subtly, but with considerable force, we're often made to feel that there's nothing we can do to change our world. The Civil Rights Movement fought racism half a century ago, but it is still here. The 'War to End All Wars' was fought nearly a century ago, but soldiers are still fighting, people are still dying. Magic, rooted in the belief that each individual can make a difference, attacks this sense of powerlessness. Each of us is connected to everything else in the cosmos in ways that are as subtle but even more powerful than the forces of modernity. We can achieve change by bringing our intentions and imaginations together with our energetic movements and actions.

Magic is even more liberating when it is a group act. Then we realize that we are not lonely, isolated individuals at all, but are connected to each other, and share our intentions and our imaginations. We can will the same things, and we can set out to achieve change together.

When Witches perform magic, participants and the working space are first prepared or dedicated to the task. Everyday concerns are laid aside and participants undergo a ceremonial washing. A bowl of salty water is used to symbolically rinse away distractions: as you stir the water you feel everything extraneous washing away. Some magicians might also sprinkle the working space or use a traditional besom-broom to sweep it clear: a practical function in outdoor places, which also clears away any inner negativity or ambivalence. The next step is to cast the circle by marking the working space and erecting a symbolic boundary and container. The magic worker will walk around the circle, usually sun- or clock-wise, with chosen ritual implements such as wands or knives. The four directions (east, south, west and north) and their associated elements (air, fire, water and earth) are greeted with varying degrees of formality depending on the group or event. A five-pointed star or pentagram, an ancient symbol of protection and strength, might be written in the air with a wand, ceremonial dagger or simply a finger.

Once the circle is cast it is traditional not to leave it, barring emergencies, until the work is done, and then only after farewell is said to the directions and the circle is opened. Next the energy is raised, meaning both the energy and excitement of participants, and also something mystical and so-far untapped by scientists. The magic worker might seek the help of deities or significant beings, although such beings are more likely to be addressed in separate parts of Pagan ceremonies. The energy generated by the participants as they chant, dance or drum, or that sourced from powerful helpers, is contained within the magical circle. Once raised, it is directed or channelled to achieve the purpose for which the whole ceremony was created: healing a sick relative, empowering new wands or drums for magical purposes, seeking self-knowledge or finding love. Energy might be directed through focused chants or minds, or by touching the sick person or ritual implement. In some cases practitioners sit in their circle and meditate, visualizing problems, questions or objects of desire, until they feel the energy dissipating. Directing energy may involve casting spells: combinations of words and actions that address a problem and evoke a carefully planned outcome. Love spells and protection spells are particularly popular. Once the magic is done, food and drink is shared as a form of celebration, to earth any left-over energies, and as a first step in returning to everyday reality. The ceremony ends when the magic worker bids farewell to the directions, elements and any other beings invited to participate, and walks around the circle to symbolically open it.

A LOVE SPELL[25]

'If you feel the need to have someone special in your life, it is far better to prepare yourself for love, rather than making someone have an interest in you, regardless of their needs. To make yourself ready to attract romance, you could use the following magic on yourself. The basis of this spell is to realize that to attract love, you must first radiate love from your soul, and to be able to radiate love from your inner being, you must first have love for yourself as a person. This candle spell will help you to enhance the love that is already within you. For this spell you will need a pink candle. Charge this candle with your intentions by holding it while you say, "This candle helps me to attract love." Have a rose quartz crystal nearby if you want extra power, and carry it with you after the spell has been completed.

'During a waxing moon, preferably on a Friday, prepare yourself for the spell and light the candle. Feel the candle flame radiating love energy into the room, then say: "I feel love around me and within me. I radiate love. Love flows from me. Love comes to me. I love, and I am loved." Watch the flame on the candle while you fill yourself with loving thoughts. Radiate love around you. When you are ready to finish the spell, say the words: "I send my love into the world, and I know that it will return to me. With love I now release this spell, for the good of all, so it shall be!" Now extinguish the candle. Repeat this for seven consecutive nights. On the seventh night, let the candle burn itself out (safely), and if the spell has been for the good of all, then results will come within one lunar month.'

Plenty of teen-witches find their 'love spells' effective: their candlelit meditations result in new relationships. Covens claim success in healing diseases that had resisted medical expertise, such as cancers which become dormant or diminish after the use of magic. Some eco-activist Pagans tell stories about how a magical ritual protected a tree or a wood from being destroyed to make way for a road. Just as prayers in other religions sometimes get a 'no' answer, so magic can fail. Perhaps the worker of magic was not clear enough in stating their intention, or perhaps they did not put enough energy into it. It is always possible that the magician's deity prevented the magic working because something more important would result from this failure.

When magic is successful some are happy to suppose a kind of placebo effect: if someone knows healing magic is being directed at them they may find the resources to become well. Others claim the support of quantum or chaos physics, arguing that if a butterfly opening its wings in New York can change the weather in Africa so the performance of a magical ritual can achieve great changes in the world. Magicians may be able to make use of some of the most fundamental connections in the universe, but whether these are part of quantum physics or wyrd (the web of life and fate that links everyone and everything) is debated. It is possible that magical ceremonies elicit the aid of generous and powerful deities, elementals and other beings. Few Pagans claim to be absolutely certain how magic works or why some of their rituals and spells succeed, but sense that magic reinforces the links between humans and the rest of life. We are not isolated nonentities in a hostile environment but participants in a cosmos in which it is at least as possible to achieve good as it is to do harm. We are responsible for trying to make the world a better place.

5

Honouring deities

Pagan ceremonies often (but not always) include invocations and offerings to divinities, although Pagans do not agree on how many goddesses and gods there are, what they do, or which ones are most important. Some Pagans scattered throughout all Pagan groups believe that there is a simple unity behind everything. The material world is an exuberant expression of an original 'one-ness' that is sometimes called 'Spirit' by those who wish to avoid gendered words like 'god' or 'goddess'. Some think this deity is beyond human understanding and experience, and that it sparked off the whole cosmic evolutionary process. They believe that everything we see – including ourselves – is an aspect of that deity, which is immediately experienced in all things. Some, however, believe that the underlying unity is a great mystery that is neither approachable nor intimate.

Wiccans often address two deities: 'the Goddess' and 'the God'. In ceremonies they may be linked to particular seasons, as deities of the growing corn or harvest. These divinities, often in a male and female pair, are taken from various ancient cultures. Ceridwen and Cernunnos, or Persephone and Hades, are derived from Celtic or Greek cultures; Isis and Osiris from ancient Egyptian religion; Aradia and Apollo from nineteenth-century Italian folklore. Sometimes the Goddess is revealed as the Earth Mother, sometimes as the shining Moon. Whatever name or role they have, the deities speak through their priestesses and priests, and become present in them. Many Wiccans consider these two deities a manifestation of the one underlying reality, but, more commonly Wiccans believe that the Goddess and the God express the dynamic polarity of feminine and masculine forms and energies. In other words, although Wiccans have been described as 'bitheists' or 'duotheists' (believers in two deities), they might as easily be observing a particular kind of monotheism or, paradoxically, a focused form of polytheism. While such distinctions are important to strict monotheists (Christians, Jews and Muslims in particular), they hardly concern Pagans. Like Hindus, Wiccans can assert that there is ultimately one divinity even though they venerate all of its manifestations.

Heathens' polytheism is far more explicit than that of most Wiccans. They honour deities named in Saxon, Norse, Icelandic and Germanic literatures. Some acknowledge the existence of all deities (even those of other religions) but pay particular attention to just a few: Woden (a wise god) or Thor (a strong protector), Freyja (goddess of love and magic) or the three Norns (spinners of fate). These deities are considered the early ancestors of Heathens, or the ancestors of all life. The births, deaths and rebirths of some deities are recorded in the Eddas (medieval Icelandic literature).[26] Their acts of creation, passion, procreation, defence and justice are celebrated. Heathens commonly make offerings to honour the wisdom, protection and friendship of a particular deity, and also to avoid the trickery of less friendly beings. In the expansive polytheism of Heathenry, deities are considered much like humans and other living beings with rounded characters far too ambiguous to reduce to neat distinctions of good and bad. Of central importance is the Heathen's formation of relationships with deities, not the codification of creeds about them.

ONE OR MANY?

An important article by Asphodel Long (one of the UK's most significant writers about goddesses and feminism) is called 'The One and the Many: the Great Goddess Revisited'.[27] Long builds on the work of Carol Christ[28] and others to demonstrate that 'the Goddess' is a real being encountered in nature and ceremony; can refer to 'all female divinities'; and might be a symbol of the processes of life, death and rebirth, or an affirmation of women's experiences. In fact, Long shows that Pagans often see the Goddess as several or all of these things at once.

Among others, Long quotes Ntozake Shange's phrase, 'I found God in myself and I loved her fiercely',[29] as well as the discovery by fellow members of the Matriarchy Study Group's that 'I am in the image of the divine', and Monica Sjöö's notion that women represent the Goddess in their creativity and procreativity. She says, 'My own formulation over a long period has been "In raising Her we raise ourselves; in raising ourselves, we raise Her".'

Remembering all these possibilities, Long says that questions about whether 'the Goddess' is a supreme deity, or one deity or many, 'actually bothers very few seekers in terms of definition'. If your purpose is to find a satisfying way to live your life in this complicated and largely male-dominated world, there are better things to do than seek definitions and count numbers.

When Pagans of different kinds meet together to celebrate a festival, they might greet significant deities and thank them for participating. If one Pagan greets 'the Goddess', the next is unlikely to say 'and the God!', or to ask 'do you mean Ceridwen, Freyja, Isis or who?' Each Pagan in the circle is likely to translate the word 'Goddess' into terms with which they are more comfortable. Since it is possible to be a Pagan atheist, one interpretation of

Goddess might be the life which unites us or all living beings. Some think the word is 'mere poetry', a metaphor to enhance the power of the ceremony.

The four elements – earth, wind, fire and water – are also often greeted as active participants in Pagan ceremonies. They are considered powerful beings which continuously co-create the world and enliven ceremonies with their presence and energies, or as symbols or personifications of the constituent parts of the world. They can be encountered as particular rocks, streams, fires, or breezes, but also in our own physical bodies.

Alongside deities and elementals, animals and plants can be invited to participate in gatherings. Sometimes birds seem to fly deliberately around the ritual circle, trees rustle at a key moment, or an animal appears to watch or respond at significant points in the ceremony. Many Pagans believe that they are being made welcome by the beings who live in ritual venues. It is not only humans who celebrate seasonal festivals, practise magic or seek to protect endangered places. We join in with other beings as one species among many. Heathens have reintroduced the Anglo-Saxon word 'wight' to talk about such encounters between humans and other-than-human beings. In contrast with 'spirits' (which can suggest something ethereal and remote from ordinary, physical life), wight refers to both otherwordly beings (such as ancestors) and to everyday ones such as humans, animals, birds and trees. A greeting to 'all the wights in this place' acknowledges both the 'spirit of place' (a metaphysical guardian of a defined location) and the living community at home there.

According to the satirical and comic fantasy of Terry Pratchett (a popular author among many Pagans), 'Most witches don't believe in gods. They know that they exist, of course. They even deal with them occasionally. But they don't believe in them. They know them too well. It would be like believing in the postman.'[30]

Similarly, Starhawk speaks for many Pagans in saying, 'People often ask me if I *believe* in the Goddess. I reply, "Do you believe in rocks?"'[31]

Paganism does not encourage the kind of systematizing of beliefs that creates creeds or dogmas. Talking about deities is one aspect of their engagement with their home, the earth and the wider cosmos. Since they celebrate the physical world, Pagans honour deities who are passionate participants in life: breeding, eating and celebrating. Since they believe in the power of magic, Pagans seek the aid of deities and other wights who offer energetic support to the project of making the world a better place. In seasonal ceremonies Pagans talk with deities who aid the growth of wheat or the heat of summer, thanking them for their work and honouring them for their presence. In magical rituals Pagans request help and guidance from deities who possess power and wisdom. The deities respond, speaking through Wiccan priestesses or entranced Heathen shamans, or showing their presence in the changes in people's lives that they experience after the ritual.

Pagans learn about deities, elementals and other wights by participating in ceremonies and by listening to storytelling. The story of Ceridwen and Taliesin (first known from medieval manuscripts, but possibly originating much earlier) is often retold. Ceridwen wanted to provide her child, known as Morfran or Avagddu, with wisdom to make up for his lack of beauty. She prepared magical ingredients in a cauldron and set it over a fire. A blind man and his son, Gwion, tend the fire. After a year and a day the seething cauldron spat out three drops of inspiration from the otherwise poisonous brew. The hot liquid landed on Gwion's thumb, which he put in his mouth. Having gained the Goddess's wisdom, Gwion anticipated Ceridwen's anger and fled, transforming himself into a hare. Ceridwen chased him as a hound. Gwion became a fish but Ceridwen pursued him as an otter. He became a bird and she a hawk. He hid himself as one grain of wheat among many. Ceridwen became a hen and swallowed the grain. Nine months later she gave birth to Gwion in a new form and, still angry, tied him in a bag and threw him into the sea. The bag washed up on a fishing weir where it was found and opened. The wise child within was re-named Taliesin, meaning the radiant brow, and became Britain's chief bard (storyteller, keeper of lore, maintainer of tradition). The story teaches the possibility of transformation, or shape-shifting, and supports the notion that wisdom can be gained in magical ceremonies. This story both entertains and enchants – important aspects of Pagan celebrations.

A belief about deities positively enriches aspects of Pagan communities. Beliefs about a goddess or goddesses contest the practice and teaching of male dominant hierarchies, and create a more equal footing for women and men. In addition to that liberation, the deities encourage ethical behaviour by insisting that all living beings share responsibility for creating the world. We are encouraged to act morally because we are all related participants in a continuously evolving cosmos. We are freed from the burden of detached objectivity and isolated individualism, and encouraged to live more respectfully and responsibly in local, regional and global ways. It is not the duty of deities alone to make the world a better place, nor are they expected to be on call to respond to every human request, but knowing that deities too participate in efforts to make the world a better place for all is inspiring and empowering. Like hedgehogs, salmon, oaks and mosquitoes, deities are part of the community of life and can be encouraged to act responsibly. Because deities may be more powerful or more wise than other beings, they can be asked (but never coerced) into participating in actions that improve life for others. They might provide healing energies or knowledge, or wield their power to prevent forests being destroyed.

Some deities and other beings are thought to live in the

Otherworld, a place both apart from and part of the world. It is possible for humans to journey to the Otherworld, but is never quite located on a map. At the festivals of Beltain (1 May and its eve) and Samhain (1 November and its eve), which mark the key transitions between the warm and cold halves of the year, there is only a veil separating our world from the Otherworld. It is as near as the inside of a tree or a barrow mound. The Otherworld is another, normally unseen, dimension. It is a place of great enchantment, but stories say that time works differently there: those who go there might not return for seventy years even though they only experience a brief sojourn. The Otherworld is a distillation of the beauty of the world, but its glamour would overwhelm anyone unprepared for such a concentration of majesty. Journeys are not to be undertaken lightly.

OTHERWORLD INHABITANTS AND GEOGRAPHY[32]

'Conle the Red-haired, a son of Conn of the Hundred Battles, was with his father one day on the heights of Uisnech, when he saw a woman in a strange dress. Conle said, "Where have you come from, woman?" The woman replied, "I have come from the Lands of the Living, where there is neither death nor sin nor transgression. We enjoy everlasting feasts without their needing to be served. We have goodwill without strife. We live in a great fairy hill." – *The Adventure of Conle* (anonymous 8th-century Irish tale)

'. . . as I gazed around me I saw a fairy hill, brightly lit, with many drinking-horns and bowls and cups of glass and of pale gold in it . . . and I saw twenty-eight warriors on one side of the house with a lovely fair-headed woman beside every man of them . . .' – Cailte's description of a fairy feast (anonymous 8th-century Irish tale)

'When they were all gathered together in the palace, they saw a woman in a strange dress in the middle of the hall. Then she sang these fifty verses to Bran, while the company listened to them, and they all saw the woman: "Here is a branch from the apple-tree of Emhain, like those that are familiar; twigs of white silver on it, and crystal fringes with flowers . . . Loveliness of a wondrous land, whose aspects are beautiful, whose view is fair, excellent, without a trace of mist." – *The Islands of the Earthly Paradise* (anonymous 7th/8th-century Irish tale)

Irish and Welsh myths say that the seasons of the Otherworld are the opposite of ours: you can recognize a visitor from the Otherworld by the sprig of blossom they carry in autumn or the ripe fruit they bring into our spring. Visitors from the Otherworld include the faery folk – not the cute gossamer-winged beings of children's stories but ambiguous beings whose visits bring danger. Like tigers or jaguars, they are beautiful and elusive and follow their own purposes and predilections. Meeting them safely – as shamans might do after much training and preparation – requires considerable care. The Otherworld is also home to the oldest deities of the land: those who established its foundations and contours and who may offer their considerable gifts of knowledge and power to aid the well-being of those who live respectfully in this world. In the Pagan view, although these beings are wiser and more powerful than us, they are as much our relations as the animals and plants with whom we share life.

OTHERWORLD DANGERS

The Otherworld is always described as a beautiful place, but sooner or later most stories warn that it is a dangerous place. W. B. Yeats, the Irish poet and dramatist, wrote about the enchanted life of the faery folk of Glen Carr, near Sligo on Ireland's west coast. But having evoked their ease and pleasure, he records their desire to entice a human child away from his home and all that he loves. We are never told why, but other tales make it clear that Otherworld beings do not always have human interests at heart. In the tales of Thomas the Rhymer and Tan Lin, the heroes are seduced 'away' (a term that can connote not only a journey but also madness in many folktales) and either return many years later or never yet. Irish folklore speaks of brides abducted on the eve of their weddings and young men forced to participate in violent versions of what seem to be sports in the Otherworld. Several of Terry Pratchett's Discworld novels, especially *Lords and Ladies* (1993), draw on these traditions to play with the sinister activities of Otherworld beings. The enchantment of the Otherworld can be a significant temptation towards an escapist romanticism, attracting people away from celebrating and fully participating in this world.

Even Pagans who belong to the same group and re-tell the same legends can hold quite different beliefs about the Otherworld. Some think it a dimension of the earth that is normally unseen, requiring a shift in consciousness and vision before it can be experienced. Others believe it has a real, physical location, which brave or foolish travellers can visit at the rare magical moments (usually at Samhain and Beltain) when the path between the worlds is open. Some insist that whenever a magic circle is cast it creates a space between this world and the Otherworld, making it possible to journey beyond ordinary reality and gain knowledge and power to effect change. Others say that the Otherworld is a dimension of each individual's inner reality – their subconscious or imaginal world – and that it can be visited in dreams or meditations. In fact, it does not matter to most Pagans whether the Otherworld is a physical, outer location or an inner, psychological reality. If it is 'out there' it needs to be encountered in personal experience. If it is 'inside' it feels like reality. The Otherworld is not only elusive but paradoxical: inner and outer, near and far, desirable and dangerous, empowering and overwhelming.

Pagan celebrations and magic are enriched and empowered by respectful communication with Otherworld beings. Ceremonies often take place in ancient sacred sites which our ancestors marked with standing stones, carved trees, temples and shrines, and in which they made offerings to guardians, deities and other beings. When magic is performed, the inner space of the ritual circle is different from the space beyond it: the act of casting a circle causes changes in space and time. A circle is a meeting place between this world and the Otherworld. Along with ancient woodlands (we might poetically call these 'the greenwood') and wildernesses, these ancient sacred places and temporary magical circles are enclaves of the Otherworld in this world. They enrich, enchant and empower our ordinary lives.

Although Otherworld beings can be passionately interested in this world, they are not part of our everyday life. They empower Pagan lives by revealing the Otherworld dimension of reality and injecting enchantment into our world. Pagan festivals transform celebrants by building and strengthening relationships between the everyday and the exceptional. They enable us to encounter Otherworld beings, and to receive gifts of knowledge and help from them, but they are not about leaving this world behind.

Whether we travel to the Otherworld or are visited by beings from this separate dimension, 'walking between the worlds' at festivals and magical rituals reinforces the Pagan vision of the vitality, richness, diversity and 'other-than-human-ness' of the world. We are not in charge of the world, we aren't always safe, but we are part of it, and responsible for living well with other beings who are also significant members of the cosmic community of life. Pagan deities are subject to the same natural laws and magical enchantments as all other beings who co-inhabit and co-create the cosmos. Deities, humans, plants, animals, elements and all living beings are called upon to live respect-fully together and to seek to improve life for all.

6

Paganism in action

Pagans don't talk much about beliefs or believing but prefer to work their convictions out in action, especially in ceremonies and rituals.

About twenty miles north of Stonehenge is a less famous but larger and more ancient circle of large standing stones, Avebury. It is surrounded by an enormous bank and ditch, still intact some three thousand years after they were first made. Beyond the bank are other ancient features that make up a complex sacred landscape. Silbury Hill (the largest artificial mound in Europe), many burial mounds, settlement sites, trackways and field systems are within walking distance. Visit on any day of the year and you'll find Pagans here, although they may not identify themselves among the other visitors and locals. Come on a festival day, and Pagans will be performing ceremonies in groups or wandering among the stones.

Sunrise on the summer solstice is celebrated at Avebury,

as at Stonehenge, with a large gathering. Some people camp nearby for a week before the solstice, others arrive through the night and wait for dawn. They introduce themselves to the stones and the ancestors who are still responsible for the place. They make or listen to music. They visit the village pub that has stood almost in the exact centre of the circle for hundreds of years. The atmosphere is carnival-like in one place and meditative elsewhere.

As the mists of first light slowly evaporate and the sky announces the rising sun, the mood becomes quiet and expectant. Some people wait by stones with which they have formed an affinity, others sit on the banks or by one of the ash or beech trees in the circle. If people are not already in groups they may now join with others. These groups include Druids wearing long white gowns, some carrying staffs, or members of Wiccan covens and their friends, often wearing silver and amber jewellery, particularly the five-pointed stars or pentagrams that act as protective symbols and proclaim that the wearer is a Wiccan.

When the sun rises over the rolling hills, it is greeted with cheers, applause, songs and pleasure. Libations – offerings of wine, mead, beer or water – may be poured for the sun, earth, deities and ancestors, and more drinks shared among groups. The seasonal alignment of the sun and the earth is an intimate moment between the two life-givers. For this reason, many Pagans choose the summer solstice to get married. Within the circles of the sun-lit or rain-washed horizon and the ancestral rings of earth and stone, couples express their love to each other, witnessed by friends and family.

Wiccans also celebrate regular monthly ceremonies, meeting in covens on full-moon nights. Sometimes a coven will meet in the house of the founder member, their high priestess, where they move the furniture to one side of the living room so that it can become their temple space. Or a coven may travel a short distance to a secluded glade in a woodland that is familiar to them from past visits, a place where the full moon will be visible. They are robed in black, the colour of the depths of the earth, sky, womb and other places of origin. The moon rises above the trees. An owl calls from the edge of the nearby wheat-field that will be harvested tomorrow. The coven disrobe and process into the centre of the clearing to work 'skyclad', naked. They have known each other for some years and their ritual nudity enhances the sense that what they are about to do is special and separate from ordinary, everyday life. Perhaps too it enables them to create enough magic to take back into their everyday lives.

The priestess leads the way, sweeping a circular path with a traditional broom, a besom. As they form their circle, everyone concentrates on their reasons for being here (the working of magic for a purpose agreed earlier), and then on the moment itself. The priestess takes consecrated salty water and sprinkles it around the circle, and over each Witch. The consecration is followed by purification with incense made specially by a coven member. In the high priestess's home, this group usually carries a lit candle around the circle as they invite the presence of the Goddess and God, but beneath the full moon they do not need the candle. The circle and the coven is now purified and prepared for their work.

Four members of the coven, also initiated priests and priestesses, join with the high priestess in invoking the elemental beings fire, earth, water, air, associated with the four cardinal directions, east, south, west and north. At each quarter of the circle the high priestess invites the element to participate in the circle, bringing its particular kind of airy, fiery, watery or earthy energy or wisdom. Another priest or priestess holds out a symbol of that element: a sword, wand, cup or mirror. Everyone else faces outwards and visualizes the arrival of the element. Over the years of working and talking together the coven have found that they visualize the same forms for each elemental being.

Visualization, a concentrated form of imagination, plays a significant part in the whole occasion. The coven raises energy by dancing and chanting, with the full participation of the Goddess, present both as the moon and as a voice speaking through her priestess. Each witch concentrates on their intentions for the particular ceremony. When the magical energy is at its height, they focus on sending it out to achieve its purpose. Visualization, raising energy and directing it are large parts of their magic, and significant aspects of what covens teach in their year-and-a-day initiatory process.

The magic done, the members of the coven close the circle by reversing the process by which it was cast. They say 'hail and farewell' to the elements and offer thanks to their Goddess and God. After dressing in their robes, they share a small meal (not forgetting to make offerings from their plates and cups) in anticipation of a bountiful harvest. The coven leave the wood and return to their homes for a dream-filled and refreshing sleep in the few hours left before dawn.

While Heathens often meet outdoors to celebrate festivals, they also organize indoor events to commune with Woden, the god of wisdom, magic and battle. On a typical evening, the group's leader hosts the feast in her dining room which has become a feast hall. The group, or 'hearth', has gathered to ask Woden questions, and he will answer through hearth member Jo. Jo, as Woden, sits in his high seat, a solid oak chair with a high back and ornate arm rests. Woden's travelling staff, cloak and wide-brimmed hat rest in the corner behind the seat. Woden wears an eye patch as he gave up one eye to gain a truer vision, achieving wisdom by gazing into a pool among the roots of the World Tree.

Jo and this hearth are part of a growing movement that is reviving ancient shamanic practices, drawing on Icelandic, Scandinavian and Anglo-Saxon traditions. In Heathen understanding our world is one of nine that are linked by a World Tree. Each world or dimension is home to different living beings, some of whom are able to travel between these places. Specially trained humans, shamans and seers, can travel – with care and respect – to the homes of the deities or the dead to seek knowledge or wisdom. Jo is a 'seer', one who sees. She has learnt how to alter her consciousness to see the world in a different way, and as she sits in the high seat she is able to travel to other places. She has also learnt the appropriate etiquette for engaging with other-than-human beings as she travels. Jo often serves her community by seeking the answers to their questions in these other realms and sometimes she serves as a medium through whom Woden speaks directly.

Woden has been offered an ornate mead-horn, brimming full of golden mead. He is invited to join the feast and to answer questions. The other deities of the Heathen pantheon have been honoured too – this group would never dream of honouring only one of their deities, even when it is Woden whose presence and advice they are particularly interested in. People stand, offer praise to Woden, and ask questions about a range of issues. They want advice about healing, love, work and difficult decisions. Some seek fuller understanding of obscure parts of ancient stories. Sometimes Woden's answers are clear to everyone, sometimes they are enigmatic and lead to more questions. One of the group stands near the high seat and watches for a sign that Woden is leaving and Jo returning from her trance. As Woden is thanked, people make sure that Jo is all right. When she leaves the high seat, the feasting begins.

Samhain is another feast popular among Druids,

Wiccans and the majority of Pagans. It marks the beginning of winter in north-west Europe and honours the dead. It is similar to the two-day Christian festival of All Souls and All Saints that begins with Halloween, taking place at the same time and for similar purposes. A typical setting might be a long beach, where two groups of Pagans sit around drift-wood fires between the sea and the sand-dunes. They are all friends, but one group prefers to celebrate with women only while the other includes some men. There is no ani-mosity here, just a difference of emphasis and practice. Both groups celebrate Goddess traditions and practices.

This ever-shifting space between the sea and dry land seems just right for a festival that honours the uneasy tran-sitions between life and death, and between the warm and cold halves of the year. Both groups chant to the Goddess, celebrating her role as taker-of-life. They consider all that they've done in the preceding year and name those things that have come to an end and the seeds of new possibilities. They acknowledge their hopes and fears. One group passes around slips of paper on which each member writes the names of things they do not like (including everything from global events to private disappointments). When everyone is ready they cast these into the flames. The other group unravel a ball of wool around their circle. When they have contemplated the things that they don't like, each member breaks the wool between their hands but keeps hold of the ends. After further contemplation, each re-ties the broken threads while naming their hopes for the future. All of life is honoured, even though these small acts of magic aim to break the power of unpleasant or dangerous things.

Both groups talk about the dead, starting with those who have recently died. They remember and celebrate all that their loved ones achieved and the influence they've had in others' lives. Some say the dead are in the Otherworld, sometimes called 'The Land of Women' or 'The Land of Youth' following old Irish traditions. Others say they are 'with the Goddess'. Some believe that the dead are reborn into the world in some form: human, animal, bird or plant.

Although it is Samhain and the veils between the worlds are thin, the windswept beach and wintry night are inauspicious for a journey to the Otherworld. They avoid speaking of faery folk in case they are drawn to them. Before midnight and the tide turns, both groups douse their fires and go to the warmth of their own homes and beds.

Festive events like these restore respectful relationships with the wider community of living beings with whom we share this planet. Eagles fly over the gathering as if to honour these people for their work. Mugwort proffers itself as to help humans enter into conversation with other living beings. During the day people pick the herb, after obtaining the plant's permission and making thank offerings in return. In the evening, as musicians and other performers entertain, mugwort tea is consumed. Some people see the light of stars or fireflies forming a web of light. Some become more aware of the diversity of life around them. People talk together about the 'web of life'. All in all, festivals blend recreation with a reintroduction to the beauty of the world. They remind people that their responsibility for co-creating the world is an invitation to celebrate and enjoy life at least as much as it is a reason to protest against abuses.

7

Celebrating responsibility

All Pagans agree that nature is good and that it is appropriate to celebrate the world, and enjoy and respect all that exists, including our own bodies. The world can be a harsh place, but this does not lead most Pagans to wish for a more 'spiritual' reality. Pagans respond to problems caused by illness and disasters by using magic to create change, or actively campaigning on certain issues. All living beings participate in making the world what it is, and Paganism encourages everyone to act responsibly and respectfully.

Although Paganism is not a prescriptive religion certain activities are typically Pagan: the celebration of seasonal festivals, the working of magic, and the strengthening of relationships with deities and other living beings. In celebrating nature, Pagans challenge the tendency of modern culture to divorce people from the land and from specific places. This feature of Paganism is almost unique in Western religions. It links Pagans to members of indigenous nations, such as Native Americans, Aboriginal Australians and members of African traditional religions, engendering a hope that the wider world might take notice and begin to recognize human kinship with the rest of the community of life.

The celebration of the natural world leads many Pagans to promote significant social change. They have challenged world leaders at the G8 conferences, opposed scientific experiments using animals or modifying plant genes, encouraged alternative forms of energy production and economic distribution, and have been keen promoters of organic farming. Far from a movement of fluffy romantics and 'tree huggers', Paganism proffers a radical vision of the world. By insisting that humans are integral members of a vibrant and interconnected community of life, Pagans counter the roots of modern abuse of the world. They do not only argue that wilderness and wildlife reserves should be protected as reminders of how the world used to be, or as resources for human leisure – it is not enough to keep the rainforests alive in case a cure for cancer might be found in an as-yet untested plant. Regardless of whether it is 'good' for humans, the world must be honoured and actively celebrated for what it is. Paganism places humans within a vast system of relationships but it dethrones them from the elite position that permits wilful abuse of the world and its inhabitants.

TOUCHING THE WORLD

'People feel "out of touch" with the world, it seems, but that world itself marks no separation. Has it ever dropped us out of touch? (Two useful tests: Still breathing? Then you are still part of it all. Dead and decaying? Still in touch.) That world, that vibrant, rich, and changing world has continued going about its business of adapting and absorbing and sliding into every niche in every new situation we have offered. And us? We have gone on hammering it, living off and not living with, pushing ourselves away from the life-pulsing beat of the earth, away from accepting responsibility for how we live our lives ... The situation is changing, however ...'
Gordon MacLellan, 'Dancing in the Daylight'

Pagans cooperate and converse with other-than-human beings about the celebration of festivals and the enhancement of well-being for all life. But the conversation is even more pervasive than this. Recent research by cognitive scientists into consciousness[33] shows that humans are far from unique: not only are many animals conscious, but many physicists now argue that matter is inherently conscious. If they are right, Pagans have all the more reason for participating in movements that seek ecological justice for all life. Once everyone recognizes that 'nature' is not a mere backdrop or resource for human use, then a new way of talking about the world will spread.

The close relationship between humans and the living world has also encouraged Pagans to to push for increased democracy. For Pagans, democracy is not just a question of freedom of religion, thought and expression, but also about the use and abuse of power itself. Feminist Pagans have explored more consensual ways of organizing groups and events. Gathering in circles encourages equal participation for all members and priestesses are trained to facilitate each member's voice in the group. Open events are increasingly common, including seasonal celebrations and pub gatherings that anyone can join. Pagan activists have argued that solving global problems is not a matter of changing leaders but of changing the nature of leadership. At the local level, Pagans have built new forms of community, contributing to grassroots live-performance culture and organizing bardic events.

The trend towards full democracy might be derailed by the attempts of some Pagans to organize a legally recognized class of clergy. A number of Pagan groups in the United States have already gained recognition for tax purposes. Some now want their priestesses and priests recognized not only as facilitators of rituals for Pagans, but as officials whose services can be employed for non-Pagans by public and state institutions (such as military and prison chaplains). Some groups want to provide rites of passage, especially child-namings, weddings and funerals, for anyone in their town or city, regardless of whether or not they are Pagans. Although formalizing the clergy could broaden Paganism's reach, it might lose its dynamic ability to change and grow if leadership is stamped with state approval.

While Paganism is based around participative rituals rather than official creeds it is less likely to become a hierarchical, organized religion. Paganism currently puts celebration first. It uses rituals to grab people's attention and inspire them to further action. Those who led the Pagan revival in the twentieth century made seasonal and magical rituals central to the religion rather than preaching sermons, reciting creeds or reading holy books. If everything important had gone into a book people might have argued about the truth of what was written. Instead, ceremonies encourage people to celebrate beauty.

One of the greatest gifts of Paganism is its emphasis on play and imagination. It will never be torn apart by arguments about whether the religion was created by humans or revealed by a deity. Paganism may be a new religion, but it works. It provides methods by which people can honour nature, work magic and venerate deities. Whether these were made up sixty years ago or six thousand years ago does not matter. Pagans are more likely to name works of fiction than academic or non-fiction books if asked which books encouraged them to become Pagans.

A paradox exists at the heart of Paganism. Pagans see the world as somewhere to celebrate, but work magic and engage in activism to make the world a better place. How can both these things be true? The goodness of the world is found in its interconnected relationships, its diversity and its seasonal rhythms of life and death. It could be a better place if humans participated more respectfully in those relationships, enhanced the diversity and celebrated cosmic life-cycles. Poverty, war, famine, sexism, racism, homophobia, speciesism, genocide, ecocide and other assaults on life are a result of the strange notion that humans are better than other living beings. Some people think assaults on humanity are more serious and pressing than the destruction of other-than-human lives. Pagans don't deny that humans are important, but they acknowledge that in an interrelated world, to damage one living being or community is to endanger all others. We should certainly concern ourselves with assaults on our fellow humans – after all, they are our closest relatives – but saving humanity at the expense of other life will not work. Humans are not isolated individuals but integral members of a network of relationships that is global if not cosmic in extent. Every being is a constituent in our community. At present humanity uses the rest of the planet as a resource or dumping ground. Ecocide (in the form of industrial farming or global warming, for example) will undermine the earth's ecosystem if we do not find a more equitable way of living.

The natural world offers enough challenges: earthquakes, volcanoes, tsunamis and so on. Those problems are compounded by the culture we have inherited and those who benefit from the current power-structures. To some degree, most of us in the West benefit. It is, therefore, our responsibility to do something about it. Paganism, the celebration of life, blends pleasure in sunrises, flowering meadows and stormy seas with a radicalism that might just make the world a healthier place in which to enjoy those delights.

Glossary

ancestors – those who came before us, who gave us life, and are still around, even if unseen, participating in ceremonies and caring for sacred places.

animists – people who consider the world to be a community of living beings, all deserving respect – even the ones they don't like.

Beltain – a festival celebrating the beginning of summer, love and desire. Traditionally, 1 May (and its preceding night) in the northern hemisphere.

bitheist – a believer in two deities.

circles – a shorthand term for meetings, especially of Witches, and a reference to the circular spaces in which many Pagan events take place.

cosmology – world views or understandings of the nature of the cosmos.

coven – a group of Witches.

Dianic (Witch)craft – women-only, Goddess-feminist groups, particularly of Witches.

Druid – a name derived from Iron Age north-west European religious leaders, but now used by Pagans with an affinity for Celtic traditions and practices.

duotheist – a believer in two deities.

ecocide – the murder of living beings and species-rich habitats (homes).

ecology – literally, 'talk about home'; more commonly the study of eco-systems.

elements and elementals – earth, air, fire and water, seen as the building blocks of all things and, sometimes, as living beings in their own right.

esoteric – literally 'hidden' until revealed to initiates; sometimes synonymous with 'magic'. Commonly refers to a long tradition of finding correspondences between aspects of the cosmos and aspects of individual humans. There are Jewish, Islamic and Christian versions of 'esotericism', the seeking of and working with such correspondences, including astrology, alchemy, Kabbalah and Gnosticism.

eutopia – literally, 'good place'; preferable to 'utopia' which literally means 'no place' or 'elsewhere' (i.e. somewhere unreachable).

faeries – elusive inhabitants of the Otherworld. In older traditions and folklore these tricksters are honoured but considered to be potentially dangerous. The term 'little people' does not describe what they are like but provides a means of speaking about them without attracting their attention.

Goddess-feminism – a version of feminism that venerates the Goddess or goddesses, both outside in the cosmos, world or nature, and inside the lives of people, particularly women.

grove – a group of Druids; derived from the practice of ancient Druids who met in groves of sacred trees.

hearth – a group of Heathens.

Heathen – someone who venerates the deities and cosmology known from Icelandic, Scandinavian, Germanic and Saxon sources.

high-ritual magicians – someone whose quest for self-knowledge is conducted in esoteric ceremonies. Some prefer to write about 'magick'.

immanence – the theory that deities are 'near by', experienced in the world and in ourselves.

libations – offerings of liquid (mead, beer, wine or water) to deities and other respected beings.

magic – derived from esotericism: 'the art of causing change according to will' or 'the art of changing consciousness according to will'.

matriarchy – women-respecting cultures. While the word looks like the opposite of 'patriarchy' it is not a replacement of male domination by female domination but an alternative in which all people are honoured.

matristic – women-respecting cultures.

mead – an alcoholic drink made by fermenting honey; favoured by many

Pagans for festivals and libations; can be drunk from mead-horns (e.g. cleaned and decorated cattle horns).

Neo-Pagan(ism) – a term preferred by some North American Pagans and some academics to distinguish contemporary Pagans from ancient ones. Since we don't call contemporary Christians 'neo-Christians' the term seems redundant.

occult – literally 'hidden', synonym of 'esoteric'.

Otherworld – a dimension of the world that can be experienced in magical ceremonies and seasonal festivals (especially Samhain and Beltain).

Pagan/pagan – the capital letter is used for those who call themselves Pagans and their religion 'Paganism'; the lower case is used for a broader community of similar religionists.

panentheism – the theory that a deity exists as a separate individual but is also experienced in the world, in everything, in matter.

pantheism – the theory that divinity is everywhere, in everything, in matter, and only experienced in the world.

pantheon – a group of deities.

patriarchy – male-dominated, hierarchical and dualistic cultures.

polytheism – the theory that many deities exist.

power – can mean dominance, energy or ability.

priestesses and priests – initiated members of Wiccan and other Pagan groups; administrators of officially recognized Pagan organizations in North America.

Samhain – a festival marking the beginning of winter and honouring the dead. Traditionally, 1 November (and its preceding night) in the northern hemisphere.

seer – literally, 'one who sees'; a person trained to use trance to alter conscious awareness and achieve understanding; a visionary who journeys to the Otherworld to seek answers for others.

shamanry – practices by which trained people alter conscious awareness and seek to aid their communities. Some talk of 'shamanism' but shamans (practitioners of shamanry) are rarely so organized as to belong to an -ism.

skyclad – literally, 'naked'. A term learnt from the Jain tradition in India where it refers to the practice of some holy people who abandon their clothes and all other possessions. In Paganism, particular Wicca, it refers to going naked in some rituals to demonstrate absolute equality and perfect trust.

theology, **thealogy**, **theoilogy** – talk about deities. The first typically refers to the systematic presentation of beliefs by monotheists, especially Christians. The second refers to feminist talk about the Goddess or goddesses. The third attempts to make the plurality of deities explicit.

trance – an altered state of consciousness.

transcendence – the theory that divinity is different (better than) and separate from humanity, matter and/or the world.

Wicca – the Craft of Witches.

will – the true or inner self – who you really are, your 'better' or 'higher' self – and the energetic pursuit of your goals.

work – an alternative way of talking about 'doing magic', Wiccan circles are largely about 'working magic'.

wyrd – the inter-connectedness and inter-relatedness of all things, events and beings. Sometimes the 'web of wyrd' can become visible and capable of being affected so that events and fates alter.

Notes

1 Thomas Hardy, *The Return of the Native* (1878); cited and discussed by Ronald Hutton, *The Triumph of the Moon: A History of Pagan Witchcraft* (Oxford: Oxford University Press, 1999), p. 27.

2 http://www.paganfed.org/

3 http://www.adherents.com/Religions_By_Adherents.html

4 http://www.statistics.gov.uk/cci/nugget.asp?id=954. The thousands who claimed to be Jedi Knights are also classed as having 'no religion'.

5 For more detailed data and discussion see Barbara Davy, *Introduction to Pagan Studies* (Lanham, MD: AltaMira, 2006).

6 Michael York, *Pagan Theology: Paganism as a World Religion* (New York: New York University Press, 2003), p. 14.

7 Results of *The Pagan Census*, discussed by Helen Berger in *A Community of Witches* (1999), p. 8. Also see Helen Berger, Evan Leach and Leigh Shaffer, *Voices from the Pagan Census: A National Survey of Witches and Neo-Pagans in the United States* (Columbia: University of South Carolina Press, 2003). (Note: in the earlier book the statistics are accidentally inflated by the omission of decimal points.)

8 Michael York, *The Emerging Network: A Sociology of the New Age and Neo-Pagan Movements* (Lanham, MD: Rowman & Littlefield, 1995).

9 Gerald Gardner, *Witchcraft Today* (London: Rider, 1954). In 1949 Gardner had written a novel about witchcraft, *High Magics Aid* (London: Atlantis Bookshop), but the magic and witchcraft there are quite different to those of the later work – or of Gardner's later Wicca.

10 You can read this – and other important texts – in Chas S. Clifton and Graham Harvey, eds., *The Paganism Reader* (London: Routledge, 2004).

11 'Occult' only means 'esoteric', matters revealed to initiates or seekers, but the sinister flavour of the word can appeal to those with a liking for melodrama.

12 For quotations from Crowley's letters and books see Ronald Hutton, *The Triumph of the Moon*, pp. 171–81.

13 Several of these sources (including Leland and Crowley), as well as Valiente's first, poetic version of the 'Charge' are included in Chas S. Clifton and Graham Harvey, eds., *The Paganism Reader*. The 'Charge' is also discussed in Ronald Hutton, *The Triumph of the Moon*, p. 247.

14 Some of these examples are included among others in John Matthews, *The Druid Source Book* (London: Blandford, 1997).

15 http://druidry.org/

16 The Secular Order also has members in Tasmania who honour that land.

17 Important sections of these are included in Chas S. Clifton and Graham Harvey, eds., *The Paganism Reader*.

18 Harvey, Graham, *Animism: Respecting the Living World* (London: Hurst, 2005).

19 Translated by Phil Cardew of University College Winchester. It is part of a larger extract from the Saga that is included in Chas S. Clifton and Graham Harvey, eds., *The Paganism Reader*, as Chapter 8.

20 http://www.caw.org/

21 http://www.paganfed.org/

22 http://www.caw.org/articles/cawquest.html

23 William Blake, *The Marriage of Heaven and Hell*, 'A Song of Liberty'.

24 For more about our sensuous belonging and participation in the world, see David Abram, *The Spell of the Sensuous* (New York: Vintage Books, 1996).

25 From Don McLeod, 'Spells and Magic', in Douglas Ezzy, ed., *Practising the Witch's Craft* (Crows Nest, NSW: Allen & Unwin, 2003), p.150.

26 See Caroline Larrington's translation of *The Poetic Edda* (Oxford: Oxford University Press, 1996).

27 Asphodel Long, 1994. 'The Goddess Movement in Britain Today', *Feminist Theology* 5: 11–39. Reprinted in Chas S. Clifton and Graham Harvey, eds., *The Paganism Reader*, pp. 305–25.

28 In particular, Long cites Carol Christ's article 'Why Women Need the Goddess', in Carol Christ and Judith Plaskow, eds., *Womanspirit Rising* (New York: Harper & Row, 1979), pp. 273–87.

29 Ntozake Shange, *For Colored Girls Who Have Considered Suicide When the Rainbow Is Enuf* (New York: Scribner, 1997; 1975).

30 Terry Pratchett, *Witches Abroad* (London: Gollancz, 1991), p. 17.

31 Starhawk, *The Spiral Dance* (San Francisco: Harper & Row, 1989), p. 91.

32 From Kenneth Jackson, 1951, *A Celtic Miscellany: Translations from the Celtic Literatures* (Harmondsworth: Penguin, 1951), pp. 143, 164, 173–4.

33 Christian de Quincey, *Radical Nature: Rediscovering the Soul of Matter*, (Montpelier, VT: Invisible Cities, 2002. Also Max Velmans, *Understanding Consciousness*, London: Routledge, 2000).

Further Reading

For a more detailed introduction to the different Pagan traditions (Wicca, Druidry, Heathenry, Goddess-feminism) and to Pagan interests and activities (shamanism, environmentalism, ethics, theology and more), see my larger book, *Listening People, Speaking Earth: Contemporary Paganism* (London: Hurst, 2nd edn, 2006).

For the history of contemporary Pagan traditions, see Ronald Hutton's *The Pagan Religions of the Ancient British Isles* (London: Blackwell, 1991) and *The Triumph of the Moon: A History of Modern Pagan Witchcraft* (Oxford University Press, 1999). For the history and development of Paganism in America, especially Wicca, see Chas Clifton's *Her Hidden Children: The Rise of Wicca and Paganism in America* (Lanham, MD: AltaMira, 2006).

For some of the sources important to the Pagan revival and some of the key texts of the movement, see Chas S. Clifton and Graham Harvey, eds., *The Paganism Reader* (London: Routledge, 2004).

Those interested in academic research into Paganism should begin with Jenny Blain, Douglas Ezzy and Graham Harvey, eds., *Researching Paganisms* (Lanham, MD: AltaMira, 2005). Students should consult Barbara Davy's *Introduction to Pagan Studies* (Lanham, MD: AltaMira, 2006).

On the internet, a Google search for 'Paganism' returns over five million links. More specific searches for particular kinds of Paganism (Druidry, Heathenry or Ukrainian traditions, for example) or particular activities (doing magic, celebrating at Stonehenge, thinking polytheologically) will narrow the list. Here are three useful websites that provide useful information and links to many other resources:

Isaac and Phaedra Bonewits' site: http://www.neopagan.net

The Witches' Voice: http://www.witchvox.com/

The Pagan Federation (UK): http://www.paganfed.org/

Bibliography

Abram, David, *The Spell of the Sensuous: Perception and Language in a More-Than-Human World* (New York: Vintage Books, 1996)

Bates, Brian, *The Way of Wyrd* (London: Century, 1983)

Blain, Jenny, Douglas Ezzy and Graham Harvey (eds), *Researching Paganisms* (Lanham, MD: AltaMira, 2005)

Blake, William, 'Vala or the Four Zoas' (1795) in Geoffrey Keynes, ed., *Blake: Complete Writings* (Oxford: Oxford University Press, 1972), pp. 263–382

Bradley, Marion, *The Mists of Avalon* (London: Sphere, 1984)

Castaneda, Carlos, *The Teachings of Don Juan* (Berkeley: University of California Press, 1968)

Christ, Carol, 'Why Women Need the Goddess: Phenomenological, Psychological and Political Reflections', in Carol Christ and Judith Plaskow, eds., *Womanspirit Rising* (New York: Harper & Row, 1979), pp. 273–87

—— *She Who Changes: Re-Imagining the Divine in the World* (New York: Palgrave Macmillan, 2003)

Clifton, Chas S., *Her Hidden Children: The Rise of Wicca and Paganism in America* (Lanham, MD: AltaMira, 2006)

—— and Graham Harvey, eds., *The Paganism Reader* (London: Routledge, 2004)

Davy, Barbara, *Introduction to Pagan Studies* (Lanham, MD: AltaMira, 2006)

Dowden, Ken, *European Paganism: The Realities of Cult from Antiquity to the Middle Ages* (London: Routledge, 2000)

Eliade, Mircea, *Shamanism: Archaic Techniques of Ecstasy* (Princeton, NJ: Princeton University Press, 1974)

Garner, Alan, *The Weirdstone of Brisingamen* (London: Collins, 2002; 1960)

Graves, Robert, *The White Goddess* (London: Faber and Faber, 1948)

Harner, Michael, *The Way of the Shaman* (San Francisco: Harper & Row, 1990)

Harvey, Graham, *Listening People, Speaking Earth: Contemporary Paganism* (London: Hurst, 2nd edn, 2006)

—— *Animism: Respecting the Living World* (London: Hurst, 2005)

Heinlein, Robert A., *Stranger in a Strange Land* (New York: Putnam, 1961)

Hutton, Ronald, *The Pagan Religions of the Ancient British Isles* (Oxford: Blackwell, 1991)

—— *The Triumph of the Moon: A History of Modern Pagan Witchcraft* (Oxford: Oxford University Press, 1999)

MacLellan, Gordon, 'Dancing in the Daylight: A Role for Shamanism in Social and Environmental Change', in Ly de Angeles, Emma Restall Orr and Thom van Dooren, eds., *Pagan Visions for a Sustainable Future.* (Woodbury, MN: Llewellyn, 2005), pp. 193–204.

Oliver, Mary, 'Wild Geese', in *Dream Work* (Atlantic Monthly Press, 1986)

Pratchett, Terry, *Wyrd Sisters* (London: Gollancz, 1988)

—— *Lords and Ladies* (London: Gollancz, 1993)

Starhawk, *Dreaming the Dark: Magic, Sex and Politics* (Boston: Beacon, 1982)

York, Michael, *The Emerging Network: A Sociology of the New Age and Neo-Pagan Movements* (Lanham, MD: Rowman & Littlefield, 1995)
—— *Pagan Theology: Paganism as a World Religion* (New York: New York University Press, 2003)

Index

INDEX